Praise for *Emotional Poverty*

Run to read this masterful collection of strategies to overcome emotional poverty! The information is transformational and provides immediate value to your team and students.

–Martinrex Kedziora, Superintendent, Moreno Valley
Unified School District, Moreno Valley, CA

Wow! One of the best/most useful reads ever. The personal accounts are terrific! At times I felt you were writing about me and my childhood.

–Kim Ellis, District Homeless Liaison, Waco
Independent School District, Waco, TX

Addressing emotional poverty is valuable and timely. Our toolbox of resources on campus has increased, and we have already seen positive results.

–Michael Curl, Principal, Cedar Bayou
Junior School, Baytown, TX

In the 30+ years I've worked in schools, this has never been more vital. Understand the "whys" of challenges you face. These practical suggestions change student lives and reduce staff stress.

–Jim Ott, School Psychologist and
Independent Consultant, Dubuque, IA

To reduce school violence, we need to focus on our students' emotional well-being, especially with students who have not had emotional stability during crucial times of development. I cannot wait to share the vast knowledge from Emotional Poverty *with my staff in the fall.*

–Pete Gleason, Principal, Bendle Middle
School, Burton, MI

A school culture of caring and support requires understanding students' physical and emotional responses. Payne's exploration of emotional poverty and classroom violence is relevant and timely.

–Karen Barber, Director of Federal Programs,
Santa Rosa Schools, Milton, FL

There are two keys to serving all children. We have to better understand what makes kids "tick," and we need tools to use immediately once we understand. Emotional Poverty *opens the door.*

–Vern Reed, Director, The Corners at West Burlington
Junior/Senior High School, West Burlington, IA

Praise for *Emotional Poverty*

I love the brain model! It gives teachers a way to talk to students about regulating the brain and emotions. This helps provide emotional stability for the students, classroom, and campus.

–Judy Weber, Educational Consultant,
Houghton Mifflin Harcourt

At last, a book that addresses the emotional resources of individuals and not the politics of school violence. It has the potential to change the trajectory of learners who might be minutes away from a violent act. A must-read.

–Rendy Belcher, i3 Project Director, Green River Regional
Educational Cooperative, Bowling Green, KY

Combining research into the brain and human development with the practical experiences of students and staff, Payne shares real tools and strategies that build positive, nurturing relationships. I feel hope that students will come to school and know they are safe.

–Jennifer Hedinger, Workforce 360 Senior
Program Manager, OhioGuidestone

Using both research and personal stories, Emotional Poverty *serves as an excellent resource for understanding how emotional issues affect schools and classrooms.*

–Sharon Ray, First Choice Administrator,
Pequea Valley School District, Kinzers, PA

Provides educators with the "how" and "why" of building relationships with students. In today's climate, we need these tools to give students a safe environment.

–Karen Coffey, Director of Intervention, Goose Creek
Consolidated Independent School District, Highlands, TX

Emotional issues can prevent learning. Payne offers educators academic and behavioral tools to create a calm learning environment and help students manage emotions.

–Lauren Puente, Behavior Specialist, Region 6
Education Service Center, Huntsville, TX

EMOTIONAL
poverty
IN ALL DEMOGRAPHICS

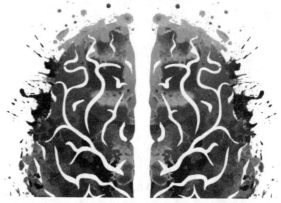

How to Reduce Anger, Anxiety, and Violence in the Classroom

Ruby K. Payne
   Emotional Poverty in All Demograhics: How to Reduce Anger, Anxiety,
      and Violence in the Classroom
   200 pages
   Bibliography: pages 171–176

   ISBN: 978-1-948244-13-8

   aha! Process, Inc.
   P.O. Box 727
   Highlands, TX 77562-0727
   (800) 424-9484 ▪ (281) 426-5300
   Fax: (281) 426-5600
   www.ahaprocess.com

Book design by Paula Nicolella
Cover design by Amy Alick Perich

Printed in the United States of America

               Library of Congress Control Number: 2018947054

EMOTIONAL
poverty

IN ALL DEMOGRAPHICS

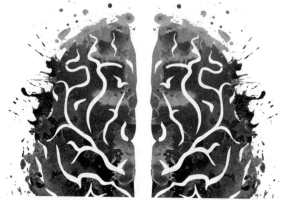

How to Reduce Anger, Anxiety, and Violence in the Classroom

Ruby K. Payne, Ph.D.

Table of Contents

Introduction
Emotional Poverty

What is emotional poverty?
How does it impact your classroom?

Increasingly in schools, educators are dealing with emotional issues, outbursts, violence, rage, anger, avoidance, and anxiety. The current methods of discipline simply are not working very well because they are not addressing emotional issues.

Emotional poverty is not a clinical disorder, and this book doesn't "diagnose" a condition in individuals. The term *emotional poverty* is descriptive of a set of realities that can surface in individuals and in classrooms and that are brought on by home and neighborhood environments.

Emotional poverty occurs when:

- The brain is not integrated or regulated
- The inner self is underdeveloped
- Bonding and attachment is not secure
- The external environment repeatedly reinforces "less than" or "separate from" status

This book explores these concepts and provides understanding, tools, and strategies that are more effective than those currently in use in most classrooms.

Emotional poverty exists in all demographics. When I was the principal of a very affluent elementary school, out of 500 children only five were financially poor. Most of the students were wealthy. However, the level of emotional poverty was high.

Why is emotional poverty such an issue? It promotes behaviors that are less than beneficial to the students themselves and to everyone around them. It can make people feel "less than" and "separate from" all of their lives. No matter how successful people in emotional poverty may be, their internal understanding is that they are never enough. Emotional poverty is subtle and unnamed. It impacts personal relationships, performance, and parenting throughout an adult's life.

So-called "deficit models" focus on something being wrong with individual people. This book seeks to identify deficits in the environment, places where resources weren't available for brain integration and regulation, secure bonding and attachment, and development of a robust inner self. Deficits also apply to environments.

Psychology frames this as a continuum of normality, but schools often separate out people who do not fit the norm. Furthermore, often deficits in the individuals are seen, but not deficits in the environment. Punishment only deepens the emotional poverty, often baffling educators when students return with violence. The school may say, "We are not responsible for the individual's emotional well-being," but the truth of the matter is that schools are responsible for the safety of all their students, and that includes the emotional well-being of students who are at risk.

After the school shooting in Parkland, Florida, Marjory Stoneman Douglas High School installed all kinds of security devices. They even made students wear see-through backpacks, but those kids didn't feel safe.

Some schools will say, "Your emotional poverty approach is too soft on the students. We need to use the broken windows theory and police every minor discipline infraction." The problem is that the broken windows approach does not make schools safer. Environments create emotional poverty, and emotional poverty motivates bad behavior. We need to motivate good behavior.

Consequences will always be needed. It is the approach that changes.

The mission of this book is to change the conceptual frame from "those are bad kids" and "they did that on purpose." Bad behavior actually comes from an unintegrated and unregulated brain, a weak inner self, and an insecure bonding and attachment style, as well as external reinforcements that indicate you are "less than" and "separate from."

It is possible to motivate good behavior.

As a side note, some problems and issues can be solved, but some can only be managed. When an issue or problem can only be managed, then the management process will require constant correction and adaptation.

A letter from Gary Rudick, former chief of Tulsa Public Schools Campus Police and current member of the Oklahoma Commission on School Security:

I've been teaching school safety and security since I was chief of Tulsa Public Schools Campus Police, and I now teach it across the country. This is an area I can speak to with some degree of authority.

Developing a positive school culture and environment is the most important thing. When we talk to kids, they tell us that the thing that makes them feel safest is not metal detectors, fences, armed guards, drug dogs, or moats with alligators. It's whether or not there is a culture of belonging, of connection, of appreciation—that there is someone here who cares about whether or not I succeed, whether or not I attend school at all, whether or not I have friends there, etc.

A culture of connection and acceptance means more to the atmosphere of safety and security than any single issue. After the Parkland, Florida, shooting, students across the nation were interviewed by media about what they thought of their own schools' safety. Students who thought their own school was safe often followed that up with, "I feel like people care about me here, and we care about each other."

Caring and mutual respect is a consistent theme in developing a safe school environment. That starts with education professionals who demonstrate a caring, nonjudgmental atmosphere. Look at the vast majority of school shootings, and you find a kid who slipped off the grid months before, isolated, alone, desperate, and moving toward revenge or to make a statement.

When I teach educators about school safety, one of the first questions I ask is:

"If you can describe in one single word what most of your kids' emotional state is, or what they typically display as the most consistent emotion, what would that one word be?"

The most frequent answer? Anger.

Kids are angry, and when you ask why they are so angry, the most common response is, "I don't know." This book, *Emotional Poverty,* can help students understand where anger comes from and why it is not altogether a bad thing; it just needs to be identified, studied, and managed. And sometimes kids have very good reasons to be mad.

I had a kid about 13 brought to my office who had been arrested for pushing a teacher. He was mad. He wouldn't talk at all or answer questions. He sat in my office so long that I got hungry, and I asked him if he was hungry too. He finally said yes, so I went to the cafeteria and got us both something to eat.

We ate in total silence until he finally asked, "Did you hear what happened to my brother?"

I had. His brother was killed in a drive-by shooting about 10 days prior, right in the family's front yard. I asked him, "Where were you when that happened?"

He replied, "I was in my bed."

"What did you do?" I asked.

"'Do?' Man, I jumped out the window and ran," he said.

"Where did you run to?" I asked.

"I didn't have no place to go. I just ran."

Throughout my life there have been times when I was afraid, but I have never been so scared that I ran from my house half naked at 3 a.m. with no safe place to go. But this kid had experienced that. And then just a few days later, we wanted him to sit in class, turn to page 35 in his math book, and solve equations.

When he couldn't get through it, he tried to leave the classroom. The teacher objected and tried to block his exit by standing in front of the door. He pushed her out of the way to get out of the room, and that was enough to get him handcuffs, an arrest record, and an automatic, statutory, six-month suspension from school.

We never saw him return to school again.

It's important that we not judge kids who are mad when we don't know what they are mad about. If we seek to punish before we understand, we only reinforce the bad behavior.

Most active shooters in schools, if not the majority of active shooters in public spaces, have striking similarities across the board. Many of those similarities are discussed in this book.

Let's start with students whose inner selves are underdeveloped, who are emotionally needy, and who exhibit destructive behavior. We see this as a precursor to those who eventually lash out in violence. The concept of "victimology" takes control of the individual. They think to themselves: *Everyone sees me as a victim and weak, but I will show you. I am not going to be remembered that way. You are going to remember me for the fear I put into your life.*

We see similar characteristics in many shooters as they move from the fantasy stage of violence (video games, drawings, essays on violence), to actual planning (gathering the weapons), to preparation (practice with weapons), and eventual implementation.

As a side note, students whose inner selves are underdeveloped are also the most targeted by pedophiles, particularly by educators who are predators. They see these kids as the most vulnerable and use their positions to gain the trust of the victim and the victim's parent or guardian (usually a single mom), and eventually they make the child a victim of their criminal intent. Add to this the fact that special-needs kids and students of color are at a disproportionately higher rate of risk, and we get a good picture of who we need to be watching out for as high-risk targets for sexual abuse by educators.

After the Columbine shooting in Colorado, the U.S. Department of Education and the U.S. Secret Service joined to conduct a series of studies on school violence and came out with the Safe School Initiative report.[1] That report emphasizes the need for behavioral threat assessment processes in schools, but most schools argue they don't have the resources to commit to the process. Even among those schools that do a threat assessment, most do not do follow up once a student is suspended.

Everyone thinks suspension is the "endgame," but it is not. First, there is still the risk that the suspended student will return to the school before the suspension is over (often because they are hungry and the school cafeteria is the only place they can get something to eat). Second, after the suspension, the student is going to return to school. How do we monitor students while they are out of school, and how do we assimilate students back into the culture successfully? Even when a threat assessment is in place, those plans for reintegration are usually left out.

As this book advocates, we do need better triage processes to both identify and serve students who are potential risks for violence, but schools need funding for these efforts. Funds to provide monitoring outside school hours would help too. If parents can't help, we can't expect kids to get well on their own. Many parents want to do something but don't know how or where to turn. After-hours support could help that.

A less expensive procedure to implement is having just one point of entry to a school. Every morning, have as many teachers and staff members as possible present to greet students at the door. This low- to no-cost process is actually a method of behavior assessment and observation. Teachers and staff watch kids as they exit the cars and buses: What is the interaction between parent and child? What is the interaction between a given student and other students? How do students greet you when you speak to them? What are they wearing? How is their appearance? Do they appear sleepy, withdrawn, sullen, angry? All of these things can be observed and used to assess the potential for high-risk, violent behavior. Students who eat alone and remain alone in common areas are often the ones teachers need to reach out to.

The bottom line here is that assessing risk and potential threats before the student becomes violent is important, and that creating a caring school culture can help eliminate some of those risks from developing in the first place. The first challenge is to get schools to create that culture of caring and mutual respect. The second challenge is for schools to adopt a behavioral threat assessment process and to remain faithful to it—even when things are going well and there are no students who seem to be immediate threats. I am currently studying the possibility of creating threat assessment teams to support schools, particularly rural schools without significant resources. Many smaller districts simply don't have the resources to pull a team together.

But every district and every school has the resources to develop a culture of caring and support, and that's the front line in preventing school violence.

What can you do to develop a school culture that prevents violence? One way to start is by identifying the emotional resources of your students. Think of a student you have in your classroom or building right now, and complete the following checklist for that student.

Checklist for identifying emotional resources

Controls impulsivity most of the time	Yes	No
Can plan for behavior to complete assignments	Yes	No
Controls anger	Yes	No
Has positive self-talk	Yes	No
Sees the relationship between choice and consequence	Yes	No
Can usually resolve a problem with words (does not hit or become verbally abusive)	Yes	No
Can argue without vulgarity or profanity	Yes	No
Can predict outcomes based on cause and effect	Yes	No
Can separate the behavior (criticism) from the person (contempt)	Yes	No
Usually has the words to name feelings	Yes	No
Can use the adult voice	Yes	No
Has parents who are supportive of school	Yes	No
Has at least two caring and nurturing adults	Yes	No
Has at least two friends (peers) who are nurturing and not destructive	Yes	No
Belongs to a peer group; can be racial, cultural, religious, activity-based (e.g., sports, music, academics), etc.	Yes	No
Is involved in one or more school activities (sports, music, theater, chess club, etc.)	Yes	No
Is good at making new friends (social capital)	Yes	No
Has at least two friends who are different from self (by race, culture, interest, academics, religion, etc.)	Yes	No
Is a mentor or a friend to whom others come for advice	Yes	No
Has at least two people who will be advocates	Yes	No
Is connected to a larger social network (bridging social capital—e.g., church, 4-H, Boys and Girls Club, soccer league, country club, etc.)	Yes	No
Student can identify at least one group to which student belongs	Yes	No
Has at least one teacher or coach who knows student personally and will be an advocate	Yes	No
Has at least one adult who is the primary support system for the household	Yes	No

Adapted from *Under-Resourced Learners: Eight Strategies to Boost Student Achievement* by R. K. Payne

Think of this student as you move through the book.

The following story illustrates a few ways emotional poverty can affect a student's behavior in school. (Note that in this story and in all the stories in the book, I have changed the names to protect people's identities.)

A story: Paged to my mother's suite

Megan was a sixth-grader whose family was "new money." She was more beautiful than her peers, smart, and she "took no prisoners." One day at lunch, she was caught with her arm around the neck of another sixth-grader, Elaine, moving her toward the wall to bash her head against the bricks.

Megan was brought to me for discipline. I asked Megan what happened.

She said, "Last night my mother paged me to her suite."

I said, "Excuse me. What do you mean she 'paged you to her suite?'"

She said, "You know. We have an intercom system in our home. When I got to her suite, my mother told me that she had received a call from Weight Watchers because she had been recommended for the program by a neighbor. My mother punished me for it, and I did not do it. I know Elaine did that. And I got punished by my mother for it. She told me that I had told Elaine to do that. And I had not."

I said, "So, is that why you were trying to bash Elaine's head into the wall?" She said yes.

I called the mother, who came in to see me. She said to me, "That Megan is so difficult and has been since kindergarten. Can you imagine how embarrassing it is to have a child like that? She put someone up to making that call to me. So inconsiderate. So manipulative. I am not surprised that she blamed it on someone else."

But my assessment was that Megan had not instigated the call. So what is going on here?

There is emotional poverty on the part of the mother and the child.

You might ask, "How do you know that?" First of all, the fact that Megan was "paged to the mother's suite" means that the mother is fairly distant from her child. Secondly, the fact that there was no sense of humor about the incident on the part of the mother indicates that criticism is not tolerated in any form—even in prank form. The mother's dismissal of her child to me, her inability to identify anything good about the child, and her refusal to consider the possibility that Megan might not have been at fault all indicated that the emphasis in that household was on "less than" and "separate from." There is little psychological or emotional safety or belonging there. These are all indicators of emotional poverty.

Megan isn't a bad kid, but her environment is full of risk factors for emotional poverty. This results in discipline problems in school, including violent behavior. Megan isn't alone in U.S. schools. Millions of children in the United States are being derailed by emotional poverty. As educators, we can't offer a miracle cure, but we can use proven practices to increase emotional resources. When emotional resources are high, discipline referrals and school violence are less likely to occur.

1

The Unregulated, Unintegrated Brain

Why do students explode?
Why are they out of control?

To understand the basic structure of the brain and the development of the emotional self, the "hand model" explained by Daniel Siegel is very helpful.[2]

Hand model of the brain

The palm is the brain stem, which controls the involuntary systems.

The wrist is the spinal cord.

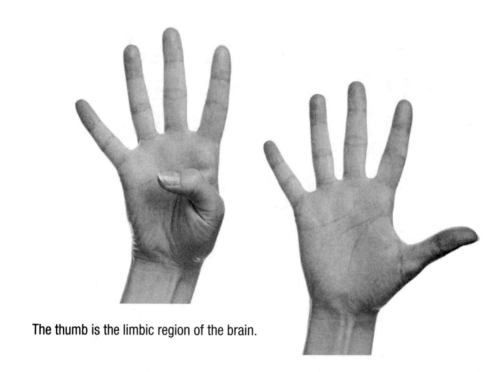

The **thumb** is the limbic region of the brain.

The back of the hand and the fingers over the thumb represent the cortex of the brain.

Prefrontal cortex

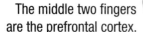
The middle two fingers
are the prefrontal cortex.

Adapted from D. J. Siegel, *Mindsight*

Put your thumb in the middle of your palm, and curl your fingers over the top. The back of the hand represents the back of your head. Your wrist is the spinal cord rising from your backbone, upon which your brain sits. The inner brain stem is your palm. Your thumb in your palm represents the limbic region of the brain. Your fingers curled over the top of your thumb represent your cortex.

The brain stem, the limbic area, and the cortex are what have been called "the triune brain." To integrate the brain means linking the activities of the brain stem, the limbic area, and the cortex. It means that these parts "talk" to each other.

This is called "vertical integration."

The brain stem

- Controls our states of arousal—hunger, sexual, awake, asleep

- Responsible for fight-or-flight response

- Identifies how we respond to threats; in survival mode, brain becomes reactive

- Is fundamental to motivational systems that help us with food, shelter, reproduction, and safety

- Works with the limbic area to get us to act

The limbic area (includes amygdala and hippocampus)

- Works with the brain stem to create our emotions

- Evaluates the situation—good or bad? We move toward the good and away from the bad

- Creates "e-motions"—the motion we choose (toward or away from) according to the meaning we assign to the situation

- Is crucial to how we form relationships and become emotionally attached to one another

- Regulates the hypothalamus—which is the endocrine control center; when we are stressed, we secrete a hormone that stimulates the adrenal glands to release cortisol, which mobilizes energy by putting our entire system on alert

- Is sensitized by trauma and then over-fires; "finding a way to soothe excessively reactive limbic firing is crucial to rebalancing emotions and diminishing the harmful effects of chronic stress"[3]

- Helps create memories—of facts, experiences, emotions

- Includes the amygdala, which is especially important in the fear response; "emotional responses can be created without consciousness and we may act on them without awareness"[4]

- Includes the hippocampus, which puts the puzzle pieces together; i.e., it is responsible for the integration of experiences—body sensations, emotions, thoughts, facts, recollections, etc.

- As we age, "the hippocampus weaves the basic forms of emotional and perceptual memory into factual and autobiographical recollections"[5]

The cortex

- Is the outer layer of the brain

- The frontal cortex moves the brain beyond survival, bodily functions, and emotional reactions and into thoughts and ideas

- The frontal cortex creates its own representations—it allows us to think about thinking

- In the hand model of the brain, the frontal cortex extends from your fingertips to the second knuckle

The prefrontal cortex

- In the hand model of the brain, the prefrontal cortex extends from your first knuckle to your fingertips

- Develops a sense of time, a sense of self, and moral judgments

- In the hand model of the brain, the two middle fingers are the middle prefrontal region—it controls impulsivity, has insight and empathy, and enacts moral judgements

- Because the prefrontal cortex is not well developed in poverty,[6] "the nine prefrontal functions: (1) bodily regulation, (2) attuned communication, (3) emotional balance, (4) response flexibility, (5) fear modulation, (6) empathy, (7) insight, (8) moral awareness, and (9) intuition"[7] are also underdeveloped

How your brain melts down

Using the hand model to illustrate, your thumb comes out and your fingers go up. Boom!

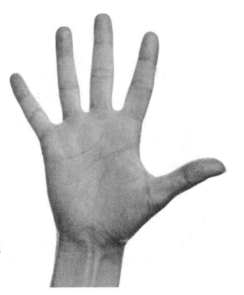

It is an in-your-face explosion!

The emotions are not regulated or integrated with the prefrontal cortex. The prefrontal cortex is the regulator. Your feelings are waving around out there unregulated. It is very easy for the fingers to fly up in the air and "explode."

> # Emotion is processed 200–5,000 times faster than thought.
>
> –Steven Stosny, *The Powerful Self*[8]

Limbic lava: An emotional response just below the middle prefrontal area can explode into out-of-control activity. Hunger, fatigue, the meaning of an event—almost anything can trigger it. The middle prefrontal cortex is the part of the brain that "calms the reactive lower limbic and brain stem layers—[when it] stops being able to regulate all the energy being stirred up and the coordination and balance of the brain is disrupted … we flip our lids."[9]

It is the prefrontal cortex that keeps the amygdala "contained within the hand." When the brain is regulated and integrated in this way, that stops emotional meltdowns from occurring.

An emotional meltdown is an unregulated, unintegrated brain response.

If a student has an emotional meltdown, and the adult responds in the same fashion, there are now two people with unregulated, unintegrated brain responses. If adults interpret the in-your-face response as disrespect, then they will respond in anger. If adults understand that they are witnessing a response from an unregulated, unintegrated brain, then the adults understand that the typical discipline techniques will not work.

So, what do the adults need to do?

1. Recall a discipline incident where you felt disrespected, then reframe the incident as a response from an unregulated, unintegrated brain. It is not about disrespect.

2. Contain the behavior so that it does not harm others. Remove the student temporarily from the situation, and begin to build in supports to assist in the regulation of the brain's response.

3. Calm the individual with an effective calming technique.

4. Teach the hand model of the brain directly to students. It becomes a mental model that the students can use to understand what is happening in their brains when they lose control. Have them label this hand according to the hand model of the brain.

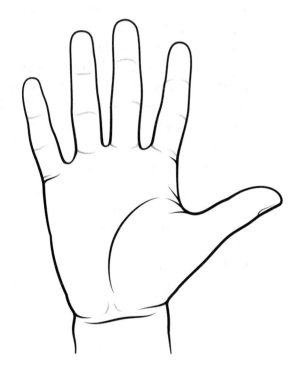

What are calming techniques?

a. **Water** – Have the student drink a glass of water. Water helps the body metabolize cortisol, which is produced when someone gets physically upset. When the shoulders relax, the water has been effective in metabolizing the cortisol.

b. **Future story** – A future story describes what the student wants to do, be, and/ or have at the age of 25. In first grade we start by having them wear different hats that represent different occupations. The discussion in the classroom is: "You have a firefighter's helmet! Now, why would you need to know math to be a firefighter?" By fourth grade the future story can be visual. Take a sheet of paper, and have the students put six boxes on the page. In the first box is a picture of their high school diploma. In the second box is how they will continue their education after high school (trade/technical school, military, college, etc.). The third box is what they will do for work. The fourth box is how much money they want to make. The fifth box is a picture of where they will live, and the sixth box is about the kind of vehicle they will drive. Then the students make a plan for getting there, and they identify the obstacles that will get in the way. At the secondary level, there are nine boxes.

c. **Tapping and touch** – Books like *Tapping the Healer Within* and *Gorilla Thumps and Bear Hugs* claim that techniques based in traditional Chinese medicine can be used to calm and heal. There's no scientific evidence that these techniques work, but the anecdotal evidence shows that they are very effective with children.[10] More importantly, these techniques do not harm children, so you can feel free to give them a try. Even something as simple as holding a child's hand can be a calming shield against an emotional meltdown. These techniques won't work with every student, but it won't do the students any harm to try.

d. **Look up** – Simply making the eyes go upward by looking at the ceiling can help calm students who are having an emotional meltdown—especially if they are crying. When eyes are up across the top of the head, the brain is processing visual information. When eyes are moving between the ears, the brain is processing auditory information. When eyes are down, the brain tends to be processing emotional or kinesthetic information. The anecdotal evidence is that looking up makes it more difficult (or even impossible) to access emotions. And it's a momentary distraction that helps students pause and regulate their responses. If you watch students, their shoulders will tend to relax as the intensity of the emotional response lessens. If you ask students to make their eyes go up and look at the ceiling, it is very hard for their brains to process feelings, so typically students will quit crying and calm down. And, like the tapping approaches described above, there's no chance it will harm students.

Visual story board

High school diploma	College/technical school/ military	Work—what do you love to do that you would do even if you didn't get paid?
Car/vehicle	Pay/money	House/apartment
Friends	Relationships/marriage	Fun/hobbies

e. **Breathing technique** – When individuals get upset, they tend to breathe much more shallowly. They tend to breathe from the upper chest. To calm an individual down, have them stand up, inhale deeply from their diaphragm, squeeze their stomach muscles, and hold the deep breath for several seconds before exhaling.

f. **Pat your heart and stomach** – Left hand over heart and rub, right hand over stomach and rub—both at the same time. Your gut has more receptors for serotonin (a calming chemical) than almost any other part of your body, and massage increases serotonin levels.

Understanding the structures of the brain and how they can be integrated and regulated is crucial. So is understanding what it looks like in the classroom when that integration and regulation fails—or worse, what it looks like when it was never fully developed in the first place.

The calming techniques listed above can help bring integration and regulation to a brain in crisis. The anecdotal evidence shows they work, and the important thing is they don't harm students, so there is nothing to lose in trying them in your own classroom.

Of course, calming techniques and brain regulation are only part of the story. If the student's inner self is underdeveloped, the emotional meltdowns are likely to continue and may even escalate into more intense responses.

2 Self-Construction and the Inner Self

What causes behavior?
What motivates bad behavior?

The motivation for good behavior is a strong inner self.

The amygdala is that part of the brain that is so critical in emotional strength and emotional meltdowns—but how does it develop? How do we construct a "self?" How does an inner self get formed?

Birth to three

The first steps in self-construction occur from birth to three. A second burst of self-construction comes during adolescence, when the brain prunes, reorganizes, and establishes new neural pathways. From birth to age three, almost all of the neural pathways are new.

What is self-construction?

Core self-evaluations are important in self-construction. They are a characteristic of a stable personality that includes a person's subconscious and their essential assessment of themselves and their abilities. People with high core self-evaluations think positively of themselves and are confident in their abilities. People with low core self-evaluations view themselves negatively and are insecure.[11]

"The term 'self-construction' is a rubric for a set of beliefs, feelings, and behaviors about the self that form the perspective from which individuals construct meaning. *Self-constructions make up the unique lens through which each individual sees the world.* In fact, the brain processes information about the world—gives it meaning—according to how it constructs the self."[12]

Self-construction builds the inner self. What the inner self does is sort through billions of stimuli to construct a world that is in agreement with the self-construction. "Although the brain is always changing, the limbic system [which includes the amygdala] is pretty much fully developed on a structural level by age three. Hence, it is called the *Toddler brain*."[13]

When you are an infant, the caregivers and key adults around you point out stimuli to which you should pay attention. As an infant, you do not know what is dangerous, how to feed yourself, or how take care of yourself. The actions and admonitions of the adults around you are factored into the development of the inner self.

Developmental psychologist and psychoanalyst Erik Erikson developed the most widely accepted theory of human psychological development. Erikson outlines the stages of development and how the inner self gets developed—both in healthy ways and in less-than-healthy ways. Erikson says psychosocial strength, what I'm calling inner strength, "depends on a total process which regulates individual life cycles, the sequence of generations, and the structure of society simultaneously, for all three have evolved together."[14]

Erikson's stages of development and the associated ages are not prescriptive but rather descriptive and approximate. Depending upon the individual, some developmental stages may occur earlier or later. Erikson outlines the kind of development that needs to occur for a strong inner self.

Each stage has a range of development that can be expressed as a continuum. For example, trust and distrust: It is possible to develop trust or distrust at this stage, depending upon the nature of the relationship and the child's external environment. People can also fall anywhere along the continuum; some people are more trusting than others, and some people are more distrustful than others.

Erikson's stages of psychosocial development

Age	Range of development	Tasks and relationships in that development
First six months	Continuum: Trust ⟨ - - ⟩ distrust Trust of others and self	▪ Mother or caregiver ▪ "Basic trust [is] the cornerstone of a vital personality"[15] ▪ Trust gives a sense of being okay—that one can trust oneself—that always remains subliminally all of one's life
Second six months	Continuum: Trust ⟨ - - ⟩ distrust Trust of others and self	▪ Focus on sensory information, the self as an individual, and the dependence on the environment—particularly the mother, who periodically attends to other issues besides the child ▪ If the child interprets the mother's absence as withdrawal instead of trust, the infant develops distrust ▪ This trust is built not upon the quantity of time with the mother but the quality
Years 2 and 3	Continuum: Autonomy ⟨ - - - ⟩ shame Shame includes self-doubt	▪ Child can either hang on or let go ▪ "For the child, controlling the bowel movement is a significant step towards autonomy"[16] ▪ Child uses *I, you, my* ▪ Obedient or rebellious ▪ Shame and doubt come if the child is made fun of, cannot reach goals, and/or if parents prove to be unpredictable ▪ Child needs to be protected from too many failures ▪ Shame is "rage turned against the self," and "doubt is the brother of shame"[17] ▪ If the child is not allowed to develop autonomy, then the child can develop self-doubt and compulsive behavior ▪ Autonomy/shame shows up in the individual's relationship to law and order

(continued on next page)

Erikson's stages of psychosocial development

(continued from previous page)

Age	Range of development	Tasks and relationships in that development
Years 4 and 5	Continuum: Initiative ◀ - - ▶ guilt	■ Shifts focus from self to the environment ■ Notices similarities and differences ■ Develops curiosity and motivation to do something ■ Language and locomotion permit exploration and imagination[18] ■ Compares self to adults ■ Intrusive—into new space, into adult minds and conversations, into the unknown ■ Develops a conscience—beginning development of morality ■ Develops a fear of losing, loss ■ If this stage is not fully developed, it will hamper and restrict initiative later in life; source of apathy if child learns it's not safe to try things ■ Contributes to identity development later in life by freeing the initiative to do adult tasks and develop one's own abilities
Year 6 to puberty	Continuum: Industry ◀ - - - ▶ inferiority	■ "Growing need to be productive, to learn something new, to contribute to the world of adults and to be recognized by it"[19] ■ "Growing abilities to watch, to join, to observe, and to participate"[20] ■ Play becomes very important—"allows the child a new level of coping with reality"[21] ■ Adults see play as a means to escape reality; for children, it is a means to cope with reality[22] ■ Can get appreciation from others by doing or learning things independently ■ If trying again is not encouraged by a role model, the child may develop a deep sense of being a failure ■ Continuous failure, fear-based teaching methods, and solely performance-based acceptance may lead to feelings of inferiority

(continued on next page)

Erikson's stages of psychosocial development
(continued from previous page)

Age	Range of development	Tasks and relationships in that development
Puberty to Year 18	Continuum: Identity ❮ - - - ❯ role confusion	▪ Pathway between childhood and adulthood ▪ Rapid body growth and genital maturity ▪ Key question is: "How am I seen by others?" ▪ The adolescent goes through a phase of upheaval similar to the one in infancy; in addition, there is the need for recognition from the outside, though for now recognition by peers is of prime importance ▪ Here the goal is to find own identity through the negation of generally accepted values and norms ▪ When there is no sense of identity, then there is role confusion; role confusion is a conflict within one's own personality ▪ Defined identity is a precondition for intimacy
Year 19 to early adulthood	Continuum: Intimacy ❮ - - - ❯ self-centeredness	▪ Building sustainable relationships and friendships; capacity for intimacy ▪ Personality formation is mostly complete ▪ Development of an ethical sense ▪ Individual can regulate intimate connections while also regulating work, procreation, and recreation ▪ If intimacy is avoided, "may settle for highly stereotyped interpersonal relations and come to retain a deep sense of isolation"[23] ▪ If intimacy has not been developed sufficiently, the consequence is often isolation, leading to psychic disorders, depressive self-absorption, or vulnerable characteristics

What does this mean in the classroom?

Stages	Stronger self-construction	Less developed self-construction
Trust ←- - -→ distrust	▪ Students tend to trust adults and see authority as a way to keep safe ▪ Tend to do what the teacher asks ▪ Tend to follow classroom guidelines	▪ Students are distrusting of adults ▪ Authority is suspect
Autonomy ←- - -→ shame	▪ I can do the tasks ▪ I can take care of and be responsible for me ▪ I can ask for help	▪ May be unwilling to try for fear of failure ▪ May develop compulsive behavior to avoid the self-doubt ▪ May see themselves as victims ▪ Very sensitive to criticism or failure
Initiative ←- - -→ guilt	▪ Are motivated to try and learn new things ▪ Curious about many things	▪ May be apathetic if it's not safe to try things ▪ May develop a fear of losing, so will not try
Industry ←- - -→ inferiority	▪ Use play to learn to cope with reality ▪ Are willing to put effort into the task ▪ Like getting appreciation from others ▪ Like to do things by themselves	▪ If no positive role model present to encourage, will often quit ▪ Fear-based teaching methods increase feelings of inferiority ▪ Will quit if they believe they are failures
Identity ←- - -→ role confusion	▪ Have the recognition of peers ▪ Have a sense of who they are ▪ Have a sense of a future story	▪ Role confusion; not sure who they are ▪ Often bullied ▪ Hard to have a future story when you are not sure about yourself

(continued on next page)

What does this mean in the classroom?
(continued from previous page)

Stages	Stronger self-construction	Less developed self-construction
Intimacy ⟷ self-centeredness	▪ Have sustainable relationships with adults and peers ▪ Respond to an ethical sense	▪ Relationships are more temporary and changeable ▪ May develop a deep sense of isolation ▪ May be depressed or vulnerable

All of these stages are instrumental in developing the inner self. It is difficult to get to self-identity if earlier stages are not developed.

What do you do in the classroom when a student appears to be 'stuck' in a developmental place?

I have heard so often in schools—even said it myself: "What is wrong with them? Really? They are 17 years old."

First of all, remember this is where they are stuck emotionally but not physically.

For example, a student who acts passive-aggressively may be working to exert control/autonomy over a situation that the student may fear as a source of shame or failure. The approach to the student would be dependent upon the age of the student. If I had a high school student who was behaving passive-aggressively, I would want to figure out what it was about that situation/assignment that triggered the student to think that there might be failure. Would it work better to have that student work with another student? Does the student have any motivation to do what you have asked the student to do?

Getting into a struggle with a passive-aggressive student is one of the least productive and most frustrating things a teacher can do.

Another example: I was talking with an elementary principal, and she said to me, "I don't know what to do. We have a fourth-grader who still makes bowel movements on the floor of the bathroom and not the toilet. And it happens quite a bit. Her teacher is so frustrated with her, and so am I."

As the story unfolded, it turned out the fourth-grader was in foster care and had been abused around ages 3–4. I told the principal, "The girl may be in the fourth grade, but emotionally she is 3 years old—typically when you get potty-trained. Emotionally she is that age. Think of the ways that people use to get a 3-year-old potty-trained. There is lots of positive reinforcement when it happens appropriately."

Who you are at your deepest emotional level is your inner self.

Why is the inner self so important? It is the motivation for good behavior.

The motivation for good behavior is a strong inner self.

What is a weak inner self?

It is when the individual sees the self as:

- A victim
- Less than
- Separate from
- Unlovable
- Damaged
- Helpless

What is a strong inner self?

When an individual sees the self as:

- Lovable
- Equal to
- Belonging
- Capable
- Worthy
- Compassionate to self and others

These inner selves become the values that motivate our behaviors.

Adolescence—During puberty

During puberty, because the brain has grown so rapidly in the first 10 years of life, the brain reorganizes, in part because puberty changes chemicals in the body and brain. The brain prunes and establishes new neural pathways.[24]

	Birth to three	Adolescence
Bonding and attachment	Is to the primary caregiver(s)	Is to peers
Self-construction	As a child	As an emerging adult
Brain development	Basic structures	Prefrontal cortex, risk centers, reward analysis, planning
Adult involvement	Critical for survival	Critical for guidance, attunement, growth
Physical development	Physical body and use of it	Sexual body and use of it

If the adults are not attuned to the adolescent—if the adults don't "get" the adolescent—or if peer acceptance is unavailable, then the weak inner self is further reinforced. Shame, humiliation, anxiety, avoidance, anger, and violence can increase. If the adults are not attuned to the adolescent, often the adults will resort to psychological control.

Behavioral control versus psychological control

Confusion between behavioral control and psychological control often occurs during adolescence. Many caregivers are threatened when a child begins to assert independence. The research indicates that behavioral control is very important— e.g., established boundaries, consequences, and choices for behavior. Behavioral control is beneficial to the child.

Psychological control, i.e., dictating someone else's identity and thinking, is very unhealthy for the development of the individual. Apathy and passive-aggressive behavior are often the results. Particularly in adolescence, it is important for individuals to determine their own identity, as that is the basis for intimacy. If a person develops identity under controlling external pressure, then that forces a crisis in adulthood.

Another huge issue in adolescence is the beginning of puberty and sexual identity. Between the ages of about 9 and 18, girls experience their first menstrual period, boys experience their first ejaculation, and bodies and hormones change drastically.

The following excerpts are from my book *Achievement for All,* which is about adolescence. It was published by the Association for Middle Level Education, which has graciously granted permission to reprint the excerpts here.

What does research indicate about psychological development for adolescents?

Most young adolescents are preoccupied with themselves and what others think of them. David Elkind refers to this as "adolescent egocentrism."[25] Occurring in both sexes and in all ethnicities, it happens in part because of the maturation process going on inside the brain.

This adolescent egocentrism causes most adolescents to have an inflated, even melodramatic, view of themselves, their significance, and their role in the world. They feel as though no one has their problems (including self-esteem problems) and that they are unique. Elkind identifies several aspects of adolescent egocentrism to include the *personal fable* (the belief that the adolescent will be famous, adored, worshiped, legendary) and the *invincibility fable* (regardless of the adolescent's behavior, no harm will occur).

The young adolescents' egocentrism causes them to create an "imaginary audience," who watches, critiques, and pays attention to everything the individual does.[26] This imaginary audience makes the adolescent even more self-conscious. What this audience does more than anything else is *judge* the adolescent—and so, during the day, any incident, innocuous or with intent, impacts the adolescent either for better or for worse—"Oh, he looked at me" (interpretation: *I must be beautiful*) or "Oh, he ignored me" (interpretation: *I must be ugly*). The imaginary audience obscures any reality checks. The adolescent, therefore, literally careens through the day in response to this imaginary audience. This self-absorbed psychological experience feeds into and helps develop adolescent identity.

Identity

Part of the human quest for meaning is to determine *Who am I?* And adolescents are no different. During early adolescence there's a strong desire to find a niche with friends and develop close relationships with them. It's part of the individuation from parents that must occur in order to become an adult. Erik Erikson writes that finding identity is the primary task of adolescence;[27] he is credited with coining the phrase "identity crisis." As this process of finding identity is taking place, Erikson identifies "role confusion"—i.e., the complicated, often conflict-inducing task of finding out who you are and separating from parents, other adults, and friends. Erikson holds that role confusion is addressed by having "identity achievement"—figuring out the beliefs, values, talents, and culture that you wish to keep as your own.

It's during this period that adolescents are most prone to argue with and challenge adults. Because their negotiating skills and vocabulary may not have the conceptual frames necessary for more sophisticated arguments, the discussions often become muddied with accusation, criticism, and blame. Bickering and nitpicking with adults become frequent occurrences. Adolescents' search for their identities is often shown as they argue, try out different points of view, and explore the areas of religion, politics, gender, ethnicity, and socialization.

There are four principal ways that adolescents deal with identity development: diffusion, foreclosure, moratorium, and achievement.

- Diffusion means that the confusion is intense, so adolescents are often overwhelmed and simply engage in avoidance activities (gaming, TV watching, sleeping, etc.).

- Foreclosure means they stop questioning and simply accept the traditional values without further questioning.

- Moratorium means they take a "time out." (For example, college is a moratorium of sorts where one is allowed to experiment with many ideas and experiences without making a long-term decision.)

- Achievement means that some sort of understanding of self is determined.

In other words, when adolescents are immersed in figuring out just who they are and what they believe, they can become so intensely involved and passionate that they get overwhelmed and take refuge in avoidance activities such as sleeping, sports, gaming, TV watching, using digital devices, etc., and then pick up the struggle later. They may choose to keep on trying out options without making a long-term decision, or they may just stop questioning the issue altogether and accept the traditional values. And, of course, they may find and understand their identity and "live" it for a long, long time or forever. Perhaps you know a person who decided they were a vegetarian, a follower of a different religion from their parents, a social activist, or a runner in middle school and then never wavered from that position.

This identity process is repeated all of one's life, but it generally first begins in adolescence.

Peer pressure, peer power, and peer support

While the family unit constitutes the foundation of the middle level student, the student's peers are essential to the student's social development. As they move away from dependence on adults toward independence, their relationships with peers moves "front and center."

According to Oberle and Schonert-Reichl:

> *Decades of research seem to suggest that peer acceptance—the degree to which a child is socially accepted and liked by his or her peers— emerges as a core indicator for social and emotional well-being and academic success during the early adolescent years.* Particularly, studies on peer acceptance during the middle school years indicate that early adolescents who are popular, accepted, and have positive relationships with their peers also tend to be socially well-adjusted and academically more successful than those who are rejected by their peers. Explanations for the critical role of peer acceptance in academic achievement have centered around the notion that belonging to a friendship group in school can increase motivation to engage in classroom and school activities and be a valuable source of social support for students in the school context, particularly during early adolescence.[28]

Two key aspects of peer relationships are selection and facilitation. Teens will join a group that has similar values and interests and, in that process of selection, abandon other friends they had previously. After selection comes facilitation of activities, both positive and negative, with the new set of friends. "Deviancy training"—in which one person shows another how to rebel against the social norms—can involve teens in actions as part of a group that a teen would not undertake as an individual.[29]

Romantic interests

This is also the time when early romantic interest begins. Berger writes:

> Dexter Dunphy (1963) identified the sequence of male-female relationships during childhood and adolescence: (1) groups of friends, exclusively one sex or the other; (2) a loose association of girls and boys, with public interactions within a crowd; (3) small mixed-sex groups of advanced members of the crowd; and (4) formation of couples, with private intimacies.[30]

Research shows that the timing of couple formation is heavily influenced by culture and that forming couples during early adolescence, particularly for girls, is a sign of trouble.

So where do adolescents learn about sex? Often from their peers. In the research, many parents underestimate or are unaware of the activities of their young teens. Teens tend to discuss the details of romance and sex with their peers from whom they seek advice and approval. And they worry that there may be something wrong with them sexually—undersexed, oversexed, deviant, body issues, etc.

Source: Reprinted with permission from the Association for Middle Level Education. Excerpted from *Achievement for All: Keys to Educating Middle Grades Students in Poverty* (2013), available at www.amle.org/store

The following story illustrates self-construction in the presence of psychological control.

A story: Seeing red

Delilah was a 13-year-old girl in the ninth grade. She was the oldest child of six in a very religious family. Her parents owned their own business, and she was expected to take care of her younger siblings while her mother helped her father run the business. She started cooking breakfast for all the siblings in the morning at 10 years old.

Socialization was limited to church three times a week—Sunday morning, Sunday night, and Wednesday night—and any other time there was something happening at the church. All other activities were forbidden, including movies, dancing, ball games, etc., but watching church softball games was allowed.

Delilah loved to read, but her mother had to approve the books. Delilah borrowed the banned books from friends at school and read them anyway. Her father was preoccupied with the business and deferred all decision making about the children to the mother. The mother thought that Delilah was not religious enough and strictly enforced what she could and could not wear.

When Delilah was young, she and her father had a great relationship. But when Delilah got into her teens, her mother worked very hard to separate the father from the daughter.

Delilah got paid an allowance for doing chores, and she used her allowance to buy a red coat. Her mother was furious and told her that red was the color of whores. Delilah argued with her mother and father about her appearance. The mother told the other siblings that Delilah's behavior was awful. When Delilah cut an inch off of her hair without permission, the mother invited the minister over, and the mother, father, and minister all prayed and cried over Delilah for her sinful ways.

At that point in time, Delilah became the servant in the household—emotionally alienated from her parents and siblings for being "rebellious," "unladylike," and "sinful." Yet she was still expected to take care of all the siblings. Delilah left home as soon as she graduated from high school.

While Delilah had psychological control exerted on her during adolescence, she had a strong inner self from her early childhood, so there was no need for her to engage in destructive behavior.

How does a weak inner self create bad behavior?

What creates bad behavior?

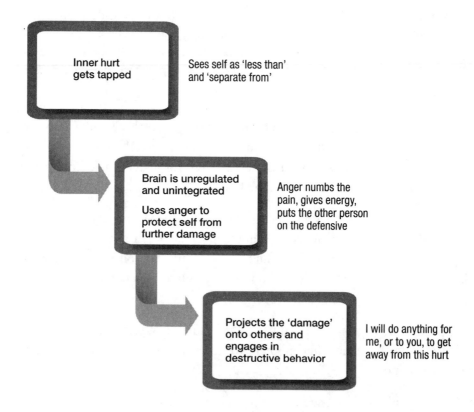

What does this mean in the classroom?

What can you do when the inner self is underdeveloped?

1. Recognize that some of the developmental stages in almost every human being are underdeveloped at some point and in some way.

2. Understand that where a person is in their emotional development is often not where they are in their chronological age.

3. Determine the extent to which the underdevelopment needs to be addressed. To what extent is this issue interfering in learning? In classroom management? In discipline?

4. Is this underdevelopment something that can be solved? Or is it something that must be managed?

5. Use the process of validation, which is outlined later in the book, to strengthen the inner self.

Bonding and Attachment

Why do discipline strategies work with
some students and not with others?

Bonding and attachment occurs from birth to three
and again during adolescence.

The following story illustrates the kinds of behaviors you might see when a student's environment has resulted in disorganized bonding and attachment. Basically, this is what you see when a child is safe and dangerous at the same time.

A story: Everything a 4-year-old is not supposed to do

Robert was a 4-year-old in a school building of 700 4-year-olds. He lived with his grandmother. When he came to school at the beginning of the school year, he did everything a 4-year-old was not supposed to do: He bit, kicked, spit on people, ran away from school, threw temper tantrums, and whipped his private parts out no matter where he was—sometimes to take care of his personal business, and sometimes just to show it off. In short, he had a disorganized pattern of bonding and attachment.

What is bonding and attachment?

Bonding and attachment is the process by which the brain becomes integrated and regulated. It is also the process by which inner strengths and weaknesses are initially developed.

The first work on bonding and attachment was done by John Bowlby.[31] Bowlby's work was concerned with attachment to the caregiver, and he focused on the effects of separation and loss on the life span.

Bowlby states:

> When a baby is born, he cannot tell one person from another ... yet by his first birthday, he ... [can] distinguish familiars from strangers ... and chooses one or more favorites ... Their loss causes anxiety and distress; their recovery, relief and a sense of security. On this foundation, it seems, the rest of his emotional life is built—without this foundation there is risk for his future happiness and health."[32]

Mary Ainsworth, a developmental psychologist who initially worked with Bowlby, came up with the most widely accepted method for measuring attachment in infants—the Strange Situation, sometimes called the Infant Strange Situation.[33]

Ainsworth theorized that a way to know that a child had a secure sense of self was to see whether the child would feel comfortable exploring without losing the sense of safety and belonging. To research this, the researchers filled a room with toys. They would watch the child explore the space while the caregiver was nearby. Then they would have a stranger walk into the room. They watched the child's response. Then the caregiver would leave the room, and the child was alone with the stranger. Then the infants were watched for their reactions to separation and reunion.

The research of Bowlby, Ainsworth, and others eventually identified four styles of bonding and attachment. Before we get into the styles, please note that some disorders may impact the attachment and bonding. Autism spectrum disorder and other conditions, especially when untreated, can make the attachment style seem disorganized when it's actually secure and attached under regular circumstances with standard interventions.

The four styles of bonding and attachment:

Secure and attached	**Insecure and anxious-ambivalent**
Insecure and anxious-avoidant	**Disorganized (safe and dangerous)**

Attachment theory asks: "Are you bonded to a caregiver? Is that bond secure or insecure? And what kind of a self did you develop?"

In the Strange Situation, when the child had **secure attachment,** the child often cried when the mother left, actively greeted her when she returned (often showing some physical response), and then returned to play and exploration. The caregiver was attuned to the child's needs, and *the child's sense of self was secure and integrated.*

Children who had **anxious-avoidant attachment** focused on toys or exploring the room and showed no signs of distress when the caregiver left or returned. The caregiver did not respond to the child's signals in a reliable or sensitive manner. In return, the child minimized activation of the attachment circuitry in the brain. *The child's sense of self was disconnected.*

When the caregiver was inconsistent, the child experienced **anxious-ambivalent attachment.** The child seemed distressed before the separation and looked for the caregiver upon return, but the child was not readily soothed and may have continued to cry. The caregiver did not give the child a sense of relief. The attachment circuitry was overactivated. *The child's sense of self was confused.*

Disorganized—safe and dangerous—attachment occurs when caregivers are unattuned to the needs of the child, are frightening to the child, and are often frightened themselves. The child cannot find any effective means to cope and develops no attachment strategy. *The child's sense of self is fragmented, unregulated, and unintegrated.*

According to Stosny, disorganized attachment occurs in about 10% of the general population but in up to 80% of high-risk groups such as the children of drug-addicted parents. It is quite upsetting to watch the child when the parent returns. The infant may look terrified, approach and then withdraw, freeze or fall to the floor, cling or cry while pulling away. The parent is unpredictable—sometimes safe and sometimes dangerous.

People whose bonding and attachment is disorganized are often very dismissive of people. Their attachments are variable: sometimes safe, sometimes dangerous. For example, when they were growing up, if they never knew whether they were going to be slapped or kissed, they couldn't put anything together about themselves, and they couldn't put stock in attachments to others.

The following stories show how a child's bonding and attachment to a caregiver can be disorganized and disoriented because the adult is sometimes safe and sometimes dangerous. The effect of this is that the child learns to be safe and dangerous too.

A story: Bad news—Dave

Dave had a father who was a self-made multimillionaire. Until Dave was 10 years old, Dave and his father were the best of buddies. When Dave went to middle school, because Dave's grades were not as good as the father wanted them to be, he started a file on Dave. The title of the file was "Bad News—Dave." The father left it on his desk where his son could see it and added to the list each time Dave did something the father did not like. Dave stated that he was so confused at that age because he could not figure out why all of a sudden he was "bad news."

The criticism and shame continued throughout adolescence. Dave was expected to stay at home and babysit younger siblings while his parents partied on the weekends. As an adult, Dave struggled with relationships; in particular, he chose romantic relationships where the partner reinforced the idea that he was "bad news." His father was physically safe but psychologically dangerous.

Bonding and attachment occurs intensely twice during childhood: in infancy (birth to three) and then again in adolescence, when the brain is making significant changes (both pruning and developing parts of the brain). The bonding and attachment of the child to an adult impacts the child's *emotional* well-being for the rest of the child's life.

A parent can be safe and dangerous in any of these ways: sexually, physically, emotionally, verbally, psychologically, etc. A parent can be very safe for the first bonding of the infant but be both safe and dangerous when the child is an adolescent and can think independently.

What does having a safe and dangerous parent do to the child?

As an infant, the child's sense of self is fragmented. Who they are as a self is not developed. As the following story illustrates, the child becomes both safe and dangerous—out of control—in total reaction to those nearby.

A story: Safe and dangerous

A high school assistant principal told me this story. The high school had a problem: Someone was going repeatedly into the faculty bathroom, putting a brown paper towel in the toilet, defecating on that paper towel, covering it up with white toilet paper, and leaving it there. The school put up cameras to record who entered the bathroom.

The student they suspected had a mother who had repeatedly—since elementary school, whenever there was a problem—come to school waving her cellphone and taking videos, screaming and yelling that she was going to litigate and that her son was innocent. This same student had targeted a freshman because she was a virgin and brutally raped her in a borrowed car during a party. The girl went to the hospital, and it was a week before the bleeding stopped.

The school identified through the cameras that the issue in the faculty bathroom was being done by the same student who committed the rape. When they confronted the student, the mother again came up to school with the same angry response. Two days before the holidays, the police came to school to arrest the student for the rape. The mother called the assistant principal and told him that earlier in the week her son and the man in the household had gotten in a fight again. She had called the police, and the police said that she needed to press charges against them both. She refused. The mother then told the assistant principal: "I am finished with my son. I am not going to help him."

The assistant principal told me: "Here we thought he was a psychopath, mentally ill, a sociopath. But now I think he became safe and dangerous to survive a safe and dangerous parent."

The mother in this story is both safe and dangerous. She protects the boy at school, but at the same time, she allows him to be harmed and ignores it. She is safe and dangerous.

Four bonding and attachment styles
(Combination of research of Bowlby, Ainsworth, and Stosny)

Secure and attached	Insecure, anxious-ambivalent
Child's sense of self is integrated and secure ▪ Are not easily influenced by peers ▪ Tend to do better academically ▪ Form healthy relationships ▪ Brain tends to be integrated and regulated ▪ Respond to traditional discipline techniques *"I'm lovable and you will find my love worth having."*[34]	**Child's sense of self is confused** ▪ Very anxious in the classroom ▪ Often easily bullied ▪ Difficulty with boundaries in relationships ▪ Do not always do the work because it might not be right ▪ Need repeated assurances ▪ Self is to blame if there is a relationship problem *"I'm not lovable, but you are so loving that I will do anything to get you to stay/like me."*[35]
Insecure, anxious-avoidant	**Disorganized (safe and dangerous)**
Child's sense of self is disconnected ▪ Tend to be loners ▪ Difficulty with forming relationships ▪ Are restricted emotionally ▪ Avoid assignments that require an emotional response ▪ Peers often do not like them ▪ Do not respond to typical discipline techniques *"I am unlovable and you'll reject me anyway, so why bother."*[36]	**Child's sense of self is fragmented, unregulated, and unintegrated** ▪ Operate out of fear and anger ▪ Cannot name their emotions ▪ Have parents who are often safe and dangerous and tend to rage when angry ▪ Few boundaries, little attachment ▪ Do not respond to typical discipline techniques ▪ Need development of regulation and inner strengths *"I'm lovable, but you're either too insensitive to see it or you're just not worthy of my love."*[37]

Stosny, a researcher and clinician, works with men who batter women. He indicates that the disorganized (safe and dangerous) style of attachment is "disproportionally represented." He goes on to say that "the most violent people in intimate relationships will be young children and young men."[38]

School violence can come from the disorganized style of bonding and attachment (safe and dangerous). In Jordan Peterson's book *12 Rules for Life,* he talks about the two young men who carried out the Columbine school shooting. "As one of the members of the Columbine duo wrote: 'The human race isn't worth fighting for, only worth killing. Give the Earth back to the animals. They deserve it infinitely more than we do. Nothing means nothing anymore.'"[39] These two clearly had disorganized—safe and dangerous—bonding and attachment. In this case it turned out to be far more dangerous than safe.

What does this information mean in your classroom?
Consequences will exist for every behavior. The approach will change.

1. Limit the rules. Clarify the boundaries.

2. Use the minimum necessary consequence.

3. Make the consequence "fit the crime."

4. Have clear classroom guidelines and enforce them consistently.

5. Interact with every student every day if possible. If not, every week at least.

6. Triage the students; 90% of your discipline issues come from 10% of the students. *Know that 10% very well.* Identify their bonding and attachment styles.

7. Be authentic and genuine. Students will have no respect for you if you are not.

8. Be honest with students.

9. Work to build students' inner strengths when possible.

10. Use the school referral system for students whose problems require the intervention of a psychologist, psychiatrist, or other behavioral health professional.

11. Above all, maintain safety and belonging in the classroom.

What does this look like in the classroom?

Securely attached children (a) meet their intellectual potential, (b) have good relationships, (c) are respected by their peers, and (d) can regulate their emotions well.[40]

Children with anxious-avoidant attachment tend to be restricted emotionally, and their peers describe them as aloof, controlling, and unlikable.[41]

Children with anxious-ambivalent attachment have a great deal of anxiety and insecurity.[42]

Children with safe and dangerous attachment face significant difficulties with relationships and the regulation of their emotions. Furthermore, many have symptoms of dissociation that place them at heightened risk for developing post-traumatic stress disorder (PTSD) after a traumatic event.

What tends to work and not work in discipline by bonding and attachment style:

Secure and attached	Insecure, anxious-ambivalent
▪ Using the adult voice ▪ Explaining the reasons for the rules and the discipline ▪ Identifying: "When you chose this behavior, you also chose this consequence." ▪ Identifying the ways in which the desired behavior is beneficial for them ***Consequences that are effective either impact loss of autonomy or control in decision making.***	▪ Helping them find a group to belong to ▪ Finding out who the student cares the most about and who cares about them (listen for an adult) ▪ Having lunch-group meetings with a counselor on what good friends do ▪ Helping to decide what they will and won't do (they will often do anything just so they can belong) ***Consequences that are effective have to do with loss of social belonging or access.***

(continued on next page)

(continued from previous page)

Insecure, anxious-avoidant	Disorganized and dismissive (safe and dangerous)
▪ Using the adult voice ▪ Appealing to an interest, hobby, or their intelligence ▪ Having them work with a buddy—someone they tolerate—usually someone who does not want anything from them but help ▪ Being honest; identifying consequences and choices ▪ They will interact in a relationship if there is a shared interest or hobby ***Consequences that are effective may impact limited access to topics/interests they like.*** *Most discipline techniques do not work with them because they have been hurt repeatedly by relationships. They simply refuse to do anything. Kick them out—they don't care. Lectures are useless. They have had a series of relationships where there have been losses—death, separation, nonattachment. **Some individuals on the autism spectrum are avoidant of relationships.	▪ Must be monitored constantly ▪ Must establish clear boundaries ▪ Must be consistent in consequences at all times ***Consequences that may be effective impact perceived loss of face, movement, or choice.*** *Attachments are often for the purpose of manipulation. Relationships are dismissed when expedient. They often bully.

Will the parents' own bonding and attachment experience impact their children?

Yes and no. If the adults cannot form a coherent life narrative from the experiences they have had, the answer is that their bonding and attachment experience tends to be repeated.

"The best predictor of a child's security of attachment is not what happened to his parents as children, but rather *how his parents made sense of those childhood experiences.*"[43]

The key to making sense is a life narrative. For example, adults whose children develop secure bonding and attachment tend to see both the positive and negative aspects of their development and how that contributed to who they are. They are able to see the adults in their childhoods through the eyes of an adult and not those of a child.

What happens when the caregivers are unable to change their own bonding and attachment experience?

If their primary caregiver is unable to do that—make sense—other relationships could make a difference. If the child or student has a relationship with a person who is genuinely attuned to them—a relative, a neighbor, a teacher, a counselor—something about that connection can help them build an inner experience of wholeness or give them the space to reflect on their lives in ways that can help them make sense of their journey.

What does this mean in the classroom? What tools can you use when there is a bonding and attachment issue?

1. Teach Teddy

Staff must teach internal self-regulation, particularly to young children. One method available free on ahaprocess.com is a series of activities that can be done with kindergartners and first-graders called "Teach Teddy." It is a series of behaviors that a child can teach to a teddy bear. In essence, the child is developing an internal regulatory voice for appropriate behaviors at school.[44]

2. Storybook

This is a mental model for use with young children to help them identify appropriate behaviors.

   a. Get a blank book.

   b. Identify, using stick figures, the student you are working with—e.g., "This is you, Robert."

   c. Identify the student's feelings when the student did the behavior—e.g., "Robert was mad."

   d. Identify what the student actually did—e.g., "Robert kicked the teacher."

   e. Identify how the victim felt—e.g., "The teacher was hurt. The teacher cried."

   f. Identify what the student could have said—e.g., "I am angry because … "

g. Identify what the student's body should do—e.g., "Feet should be on the floor."

h. Identify how the student will feel if the student is doing the behavior correctly—e.g., "Robert is calm."

i. Identify how the victim will feel if the student is doing the behavior correctly—e.g., "The teacher is calm."

Then have the student read over the pictures until the student can tell the story from the pictures. When the student does the behavior, you present the book and tell the student to read it until the student can behave appropriately. If the behavior is not in the book, someone (principal, counselor) draws it in the book and makes sure the student can tell the story from the pictures before the student leaves the office.[45]

3. Loss and gain activity

Think about a significant loss that has affected your life/relationships. Write about it.

My loss was:
It happened (when):
When I think about it, I feel:
I felt sad/angry/happy/other because …
My gain was:
What I would have liked to have expressed:
I shared my loss with/I did not share my loss with …

From *How Much of Yourself Do You Own?* by R. K. Payne and E. O'Neill-Baker

4. Reframing

Reframing is a technique used to identify the behavior that is compatible with identity. It requires the adult voice. It doesn't work if the person has a biochemical issue or addiction, and it must be framed against the individual's identity. An example is physical fighting.

Many students physically fight because it is seen as a position of strength. If you reframe it this way—"It takes more strength to stay out of a fight than get into it"—you have reframed it effectively. When parents tell me that they have told their child to fight, I thank them for giving the child necessary survival skills for their environment. Then I ask them this question: "Do you fight at work?" What you are trying to get the parent to see is that there is an appropriate place to physically fight, and it isn't school or work.

Things to say to help reframe a situation include:

- This behavior (not fighting) will help you win more often.
- This will keep you from being cheated.
- This will help you be tougher or stronger.
- This will make you smarter.
- This will help keep the people you love safe.
- This will give you power, control, and respect.
- This will keep you safer.

A coach south of Houston told me this story: The coaches had a rule that anyone who was late to class owed them a minute of push-ups for every minute late. A 10th-grade boy was late. The coach said, "Give me a minute of push-ups."

The boy said, "No way." He got sent to the office and received 45 minutes of detention.

The next day the coach said to the boy, "I didn't understand why you gave up a minute for 45 minutes." The boy was confused, so the coach said, "Yesterday, you could have done a minute of push-ups, but you chose 45 minutes of detention. I don't understand."

The day after that the boy came to the coach and said, "I'll do push-ups next time."

The coach had reframed the situation, not as power and control, but as use of time.[46]

5. Metaphor story

Another technique for working with students and adults is to use metaphor stories. A metaphor story will help an individual voice issues that affect subsequent actions. A metaphor story doesn't have any proper names in it and goes like this:

Jennifer, a student, keeps going to the nurse's office two or three times a week. There is nothing wrong with her. Yet she keeps going. An adult says to her, "Jennifer, I am going to tell a story, and I need you to help me. It's about a fourth-grade girl much like yourself. I need you to help me tell the story because I'm not in fourth grade.

"Once upon a time there was a girl who went to the nurse's office. Why did the girl go to the nurse's office? (Because she thought there was something wrong with her.) The girl went to the nurse's office because she thought there was something wrong with her. Did the nurse find anything wrong with her? (No, the nurse did not.) The nurse didn't find anything wrong with her, yet the girl kept going to the nurse. Why did the girl keep going to the nurse? (Because she thought there was something wrong with her.) So, the girl thought something was wrong with her. Why did the girl think there was something wrong with her? (She saw a TV show ...)"

The story continues until the reason for the behavior is found, and then the story needs to end on a positive note: *"She went to the doctor, and the doctor gave her tests and found that she was okay."*

This is an actual case. What came out in the story was that Jennifer had seen a TV show in which a girl her age had died suddenly and had never known she was ill. Jennifer's parents took her to the doctor, and the doctor ran tests and told Jennifer she was fine. After that, she didn't go to the nurse's office anymore.

A metaphor story is to be used one-on-one when there is a need to understand the existing behavior and motivate the student to implement the appropriate behavior.[47]

6. Drawing

7. Writing in a journal

8. Naming emotions (using emoji)

Teach words for feelings as a way to label emotions and to replace nonverbals in casual register. Boys in particular are often at a loss for words when it comes to expressing their feelings—and tuning in to the feelings of others.

Have students download emoji and match them with words for feelings.[48]

Surprised   **Hostile**   **Sad**

4 Weak Bonding and Attachment

How does feeling 'less than' and 'separate from' create anger, anxiety, avoidance, resentment, shame, guilt, humiliation, violence, and revenge?

When bonding and attachment is not secure and the inner self is weak, then the brain is not integrated and regulated. The result may be anger, anxiety, rage, revenge, and violence.

There is a process that is repeated over and over again in life. It is a process of bonding, then separation, then individuation, and then new bonding. The infant bonds to the caregiver, then the child turns two years old and the answer to everything is suddenly "no" (this is separation). Then the child learns to be an individual person in relationship to another person—develops a sense of self (this is individuation). Then the child moves on to new friends. This process repeats in adolescence, in early adulthood, and all through life.

The repeat process of life: Bonding, separation, individuation

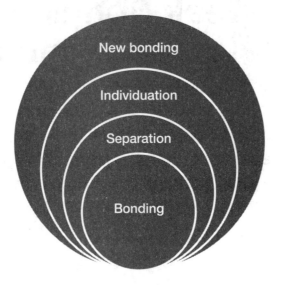

Wherever there is a white line around the circle, this indicates there is emotional work to do. If the separations come too fast or are initiated by someone else, then the necessary grieving and mourning does not happen. Instead it becomes compound grief.

When the grief work does not happen, over time one becomes "boxed in."

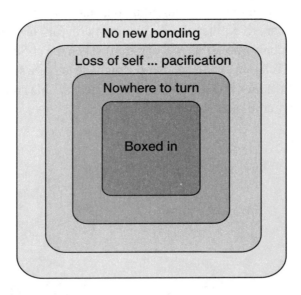

This is where anger, resentment, violence, revenge, addiction, and anxiety begin to play key roles in the person's everyday life.

Anger
What causes anger?

According to Bowlby, anger is based upon fear and is a response to separation, grief, and loss.[49]

What are the benefits of anger?

Stosny indicates that anger has benefits for the person who is angry, including:

1. It is an analgesic (numbs the pain).

2. It is an amphetamine (provides energy).

3. It allows one to seize power "by energizing behavior, advertising potency and determination, and by overriding feelings of anxiety, vulnerability, and ego threat."[50]

4. It protects the inner self from more harm.

5. It provides moral justification and validation.

6. It provides temporary relief from self-ache.

7. It provides a way to deal with fear.

Why does the brain go to the negative first?

1. Negative emotions produce greater effects. Survival often requires immediate response. Anger, fear, disgust, and distress are often related to survival.

2. Loss is always more powerful and stays in memory longer than gain. If you win $1,000, you are happy. If you lose $1,000, you remember it for a long time.

3. "Signal retreat" keeps our emotions from overwhelming us. Signal retreat means that emotions become weaker over time. It is not possible to hold on to the intensity of an emotion that is always occurring. Over time that feeling becomes the norm.

Why does the intensity of the feeling matter?

Often the intensity is related to self-validation. Intensity can occur when the brain goes straight from possibility to probability. *I know I am right even if I am wrong!*

According to Stosny, individuals can become addicted to anger. If you are dealing with a person who is addicted to anger, often the anger is used as a buffer to keep from experiencing further damage to the inner self. Abusive spouses

> convert feelings of vulnerability into anger and rage, blaming their shame and vulnerability on their attachment figures, against whose perceived assaults they feel compelled to defend themselves ... Anger used in this way—as a mechanism of externalization—serves an important protective function, guarding an already bruised or damaged or defective self from further assault of guilt, shame, and abandonment/engulfment anxiety.[51]

What can you do when a student is angry? After you use calming techniques, follow up with this:

1. Try to find out what the fear is. Fear comes from separation, grief, or loss. Underneath anger is always fear. Put the fear on a continuum of possibility to probability with a scale of 1–10. How probable is it that this fear will actually happen?

2. When there is anger, the words *should* and *ought* are almost always involved. What is the *should* or the *ought* that is surfacing in this conversation?

3. It is not possible to be angry and compassionate at the same time. Anger is an attack emotion. Compassion is an approach emotion. Show compassion *for the feelings, not the behavior.*

4. Use validation to decrease the anger and *change the motivation for the behavior.*

Anxiety
Anxiety is about fear, uncertainty, and discomfort.

When people are anxious, they are engaging in "what if" thinking. Uncertainty and discomfort occur when there is worry about safety, belonging, and acceptance. Anxious parents tend to produce anxious children.[52]

Affluence can breed anxiety. High-income households produce a significant number of highly anxious students.

Why? New money has this problem. The parents have the money to get their children the opportunities they want for them, but they do not have the connections. When you have the money but not the connections, then the only way you can have that opportunity is to be better than others. The level of competition is very high.

Suniya Luthar at Arizona State University "has found that privileged youths are among the most emotionally distressed young people in America."[53]

Furthermore, in affluence, one of the hidden rules is that it is not okay not to be perfect. Social exclusion is the weapon of choice used against people who are seen as less than perfect.

Anxiety is almost always about belonging. For example, if a student's grades are not high enough, then they cannot get into a certain college or university, and that means they cannot be with their friends. Concerns like this are common causes of anxiety among the children of the well-to-do. A high school I worked with in a wealthy Chicago neighborhood had about five students per week (out of a student body of 1,500) wind up in psychiatric institutions. Many affluent students are prescribed anti-anxiety medication, especially those who are already taking amphetamines like Adderall to stay competitive with their peers.

What can you do when a student is anxious?

1. Similar to the exercise to deal with anger, find out the what-ifs inside the student's head. Put the what-ifs on a scale of 1–10. Examine how likely it is that a particular what-if will occur.

2. Anxious students need reassurance, procedures, and markers. Markers are indicators that the work is going to be okay.

3. Anxious students often work better when they can work with a partner.

Avoidance

Avoidance is a behavioral attempt to deal with a negative emotion. It is often related to rejection and is an attack emotion. When you have students who avoid work, they often have no hope, interest, or joy in the people around them. There often is not any value seen in learning because it is not related to an emotional payoff. It may even require interacting with another human being who is seen as having little value.

One of the tools I use for avoidant students is to have them work one-on-one with another student so that they have to interact with someone. Avoidant students are often intelligent but have little motivation to interact with others. Having them work with one other student allows them to learn and participate without too much complaining.

We will discuss gender differences in more depth later, but it should be noted that female brains will engage in behaviors that will lessen fear. Male brains will engage in behaviors that avoid shame.[54]

Shame, humiliation, guilt

These three words are often used interchangeably and without clarity.

Shame is about identity, about who you are.

Humiliation occurs when criticism or contempt is added to shame.

Guilt is about something you have done.

Shame occurs when you are found to be uninteresting, unattractive, less than, separate from. One of the societal issues that happens if a person is a minority is that the dominant culture will make distinctions and separations based upon the difference as opposed to focusing on the similarities.

Shame is very difficult, if not impossible, to address unless the person experiencing shame can name the specific reality that is happening.

Humiliation occurs when criticism or contempt is added to the shame, e.g., "You are not good because you are ... " *Criticism is about the behavior. Contempt is about the person.* If the contempt or criticism comes when you are young or in your adolescence, then your inner self may be weak. If there is no adult who is compassionate to you and cares about you, then your inner self may become the motivation for undesirable behaviors.

Guilt is about something you do for which you can ask forgiveness.

What develops shame, guilt, and humiliation?

When the adults do not provide predictable safety and belonging, then the child usually concludes that there is something wrong with the child (anxiety), dismisses the attachment to the adult (avoidance), or becomes fragmented and distorted (safe and dangerous). All of these are sources of shame because the child has to choose an attachment for survival. As a result, the child cannot see the adult as faulty but rather sees the self as faulty. Children in these situations assume that they are "less than" and "separate from" the adult and others.

What are factors that may increase shame in students? That make students feel 'less than' or 'separate from?'

Shame occurs as a result of feeling less than or separate from the majority of the group. In a previous chapter we used Erikson's developmental stages to highlight driving questions for each phase of the life cycle. During adolescence and throughout adulthood, the driving question is: "How do others see me?" When the answer is assumed to be or confirmed to be uninteresting, less than, or separate from, a sense of shame may develop.

What follows is a series of stories about the kinds of issues that may increase shame. These include discrimination based on race, sexual orientation, disability, a parent with a drug addiction or mental illness, not speaking the dominant language of the country of residence, high mobility, foster care, and countless other factors.

When the inner self is weak and the end result is violence, this may be the progression from 'less than' and 'separate from' to avoidable incidents.

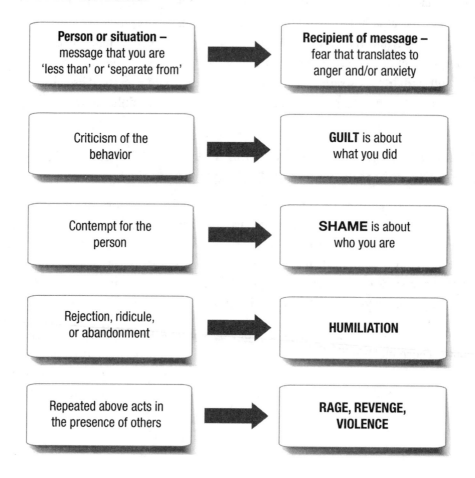

Double consciousness: Dealing with racial discrimination

by Dr. Chestin Auzenne-Curl, Qualitative Research Associate

W. E. B. Du Bois noted the complexity of developing and maintaining a single identity in the concept of "double consciousness." In reflecting on being black in America at the turn of the 20th century, Du Bois saw segregation and violence committed towards blacks. The traumas played out as a range of emotions: fear, defiance, and anxiety, among others. Being black was a large part of these Americans' identities, and with it came pressures, sensitivities, and often feelings of being less than or separate from mainstream or white America. The double consciousness highlights that while blacks were indeed Americans, they carried the stigma of "otherness" as well.

Being a racial minority is one type of otherness that can cause separations in society. Judgments, prejudices, and distinctions based on the color of an individual's skin may surface when one group is dominant and doesn't accept individuals' unique identities and cultures as another reality to be explored (though not necessarily adopted).

The idea of the double consciousness recognizes that individuals can carry with them their own view of themselves while also carrying the view of themselves as they feel others perceive them. This can be a source of stress on its own. Simply put, the hidden rules and values of any given group can cause anxiety and result in shame for others from outside that group. In these cases, not being "other" is a privilege. But there are many types of privilege to be explored, and many types of otherness.

Black, white, and green: A story of racism and classism in elementary school

When I was in the second grade, I attended a school that was for the most part white and for the most part solidly upper middle class—the kind of middle class that appreciates name-brand clothing and ribbons and bows that match socks and shoes. And there was one little girl in class who didn't fit the bill: Amy. She was usually alone, but she was very nice, so I befriended her.

We would sit together at lunch and play together at recess. Then one day she said she wanted to visit my home. I told her that I wouldn't be able to ask my mother if she could come over until I had met her mother. She got excited because her mother was going to be attending the class's Valentine's Day party.

I waited for the day to come.

When it did, I saw her mother enter the room and immediately approached her, introduced myself, and extended my hand. She did not extend her hand in return. She told me that she was sick.

I recognized the lie.

I walked back across the room to the table where Amy was sitting, and we continued our routine and enjoyed the Valentine's Day party together. However, I scanned the room and followed Amy's mother periodically. I watched her as she shook hands with and hugged other classmates. I wondered why I wasn't worthy of a handshake. What had I not done correctly? I almost asked Amy, but I didn't think she knew.

It would be our last day of friendship.

She went home, and something happened. When she returned to school the following day, she came up to me and said, "We can't be friends anymore because brown people are not allowed at my house."

Even at the age of eight, I was more concerned for Amy than I was for myself. I learned two lessons from that relationship: Lesson No. 1 one was that some people placed value on race, on color, on class. Coming from a family of many different colors, many different textures of hair, and many different sets of beliefs, I never thought about the differences being weighted. I was taught to appreciate differences and to accept them.

The second lesson wasn't as clear to me at first, but as time went on, I understood more and more about Amy's mother. She had been ostracized by all of the other mothers who felt they were higher class than was she. She needed to shield her shame by feeling better than someone, and so she chose me. More specifically, she chose my blackness.

In her eyes I was just a little brown child, but I know she found it hard to ignore my long pigtails crowned with bows, top-brand clothing, and other material things that she couldn't afford to provide for her daughter. I wondered if she knew that the other kids in class referred to Amy as poor white trash. Was it better for her to endure that alone than to have a friend of color?

After that I would still see Amy on the playground, but from a distance I noticed things I didn't notice when we were playing together. I noticed her dirty T-shirts and her tennis shoes with frayed shoestrings. I noticed that she wore the same blue jeans every day. And I noticed that she was alone.

The shame she would carry for the rest of our school years was apparent. We passed one another in the halls in high school, and she looked at the lockers instead of me. Or down at the ground when it was time for lunch. I saw her many times. And every time, she was alone.

Comments and actions that can increase shame:

1. Ignoring the individual: When we craft or adopt a single story for any group, we negate the importance of the individual's experience— experiences that form self. This is true for race, class, gender, sexuality, and many more categorizable differences.

2. Avoiding discussions of differences: Pretending that everyone is the same is dangerous. When it becomes obvious that an individual does not fit the mold, ostracism, shame, and devaluation of self can result.

3. Differential contact: When others notice that eye contact, handshakes, or hugs are given to certain individuals, those who do not receive the same treatment are distinguished from those who do.

Comments and actions that promote inner strength:

1. Honor the individual. Afford individuals authority over their stories.

2. Learn about perceptions and experiences that you do not own. If you have questions about experiences that are outside your own, research them formally or through informal discussion. Do so respectfully and without the whole group to avoid any further separation and embarrassment. Do not explain on behalf of the individual.

3. Be consistent and equitable. Individuals feel safe and included when there is a single set of rules that applies to everyone. They will notice differential treatment.

Dealing with the death of a parent

by Jim Littlejohn, Independent Education Consultant, PEACE Skills

During summer break from school, myself, my younger brother, and two younger sisters were anticipating the arrival of our newest sibling. My mother was pregnant with her fifth child and was having some complications with her pregnancy. She was taken to the hospital and had a miscarriage, and the next day she passed away from complications of the miscarriage.

All of us were in shock and dismay from this traumatic event.

I was the oldest, at 12, and I was told by the adults in our extended family that I had to be strong and help to take care of my siblings. No one explained what being strong meant, so I took my cues from the adults who attended the viewing, funeral, and/or wake that followed.

My stepfather, who truly loved my mother, did not cry. None of the men cried. I assumed being strong meant "don't cry," so I didn't cry either.

As summer progressed, my dad became more and more agitated, and everything I did was wrong. His "tough love" method of discipline was implemented through more applications of tough than love. I now know that he could not cope with the loss of his wife, and he battled depression and soothed his pain by using alcohol. This exacerbated my relationship with him and drove me to become more isolated and internalize my grief.

Two other significant events had a major impact on me that summer. The first one was when our minister came to visit us a few weeks after the funeral. While having a conversation with me, he said, "You know, your mother is in a better place."

I wanted to scream at him, "You don't know that my mother is in a better place because the best place she can be is with us!" I did not go back to church or Sunday school after that, and for the longest time I questioned the role of religion.

The second event occurred when I went back to school. It is challenging enough to move from elementary school to junior high school, but to make this transition without the guidance and support of your parents makes it more difficult. The first day back at school was about filling out forms with our parents' names and information … in every class! Some of the teachers had us write about all the fun things we did over the summer. I had nothing to write.

The afternoon math class was different. The teacher, who had a reputation for being tough, gave us a pretest on some of the content we would be learning. I put my name on the paper but did not answer any questions. I really did not want to be in school. The next day in math class, the teacher handed out the papers to all the students, and when she got to me, she balled the paper up, threw it on my desk, and told me she was going to call my mother and have her come up there because I was going to do the work in her class.

With absolutely no thought about the consequences and with my best casual register, I told her to "go f--k herself" and that if she could bring my mother back, she would be a "f--king miracle worker."

I was quickly sent to the office and given a week's suspension.

When I got home, I told my dad what happened, and after paying the price for being suspended, I was told to apologize to the teacher. I asked him if he would get me out of her class, and he said, "F--k no. You have to learn how to deal with difficult situations without cussing."

The physical punishment for getting suspended didn't sting nearly as much as the hypocrisy did.

When I went back to school the next week, I had to meet with the principal for a debriefing. He said I needed to apologize to the teacher for cursing.

I said, "I will, but don't you think she should apologize to me?"

He said, "No way. She didn't tell you to 'go f--k yourself.' Go over there and apologize. Now." I asked him if I could move to another math class, and he said no, I needed to learn how to deal with difficult situations.

I did as was requested and went to apologize to the teacher. I told her I was sorry for what I said, and she said, "I should not have balled up your paper, and I am sorry about your mother's passing. I know how you feel."

I really thought she understood me and where I was coming from, so I said to her, "I am sorry you lost your mother."

She replied, "Oh, my mother isn't dead. She's fine."

I spent the rest of the year in that math class doing nothing. The teacher's efforts to be empathetic were in my mind pathetic, and I did not want anything to do with her. Teachers have the ability to build relationships or destroy them with a sentence or two.

'Less than' and 'separate from': Creation of shame

As I look back at these events that took place during my preteen years, I recognize the extreme pain I was feeling. There was no one to help me heal or soothe the pain, but the expectation of the adults was for me to help my siblings deal with their pain. Stosny identifies this as "inner ache." The weak modes of self were dominating my life.[55]

The adult males in my life did not show any outward emotions. They separated their inner pain from any outward display. My interpretation of their behavior was that I should not cry or show emotions because if I did, I would be viewed as weak, and the shame of being perceived as weak was more than I could handle. "Real men don't cry" was the implicit message.

My angry outburst at the teacher was a result of my feeling less than adequate to cope with any conversation that was about my mom. If I had cried when the teacher said she would talk to my mom, I would have been weak. You show no pain. My encounters with the principal and the minister reinforced my internal perception that there must be something wrong with me. If I can't handle someone talking about my mom without getting emotional, then I must be less than a real man. I was not going to let that happen.

If a student has lost a parent, these kinds of comments may increase shame:

1. I am going to call your mother or father.
2. Why wasn't your mother or father at the parent-teacher conference?
3. Have your mother help you.
4. Why isn't this signed by your mother?
5. I know how you feel. (Unless you have lost a parent, please do not use this phrase.)
6. What would your parents think about this? (Examples are bad behavior or poor academic performance.)
7. What will your mom say when I tell her how you are behaving? About how you are performing in class?

These kinds of comments may help develop a strong inner self:

1. I deeply respect your strength. How can I support you?
2. Is there another adult who is there for you at this time?
3. What or who helps you deal with this loss?
4. I can only imagine what that must feel like to lose _____.

The biggest closet I lived in: Dealing with discrimination based on sexual orientation

by Anonymous

Growing up in a small town has both its blessings and curses. Everybody knows everybody, and everybody also knows your family history. As a result, the support systems are consistent, intimate, tightly woven, and rich in their past.

Along with that comes the inevitable gossip trail. Gossip itself is a double-edged sword. Sometimes gossip is shared for a common concern over someone's well-being. Sometimes it is shared for entertainment. In my experience, when someone in a tight-knit community is gay, the gossip serves both purposes. It is spoken to show pity or empathy for the family of the person who is gay. It is also spoken to show judgment and condemnation of the one who is gay. The reality of growing up in such a community compelled me to be silent and consequently fearful.

As far back as first grade, I knew I was not like the other boys, but I didn't understand why or how. All I knew was that I had traits and mannerisms that were often the punch line of someone's joke. The ridicule and harsh judgment were not restricted to the school environment. They were also in my home and in my church. Consequently, I was only safe when I was alone.

There was always a tremendous outpouring of love for me and my family, but I continuously felt compelled to keep everyone at arm's length no matter how intense their affection. The love-hate relationship I learned to have with myself was pretty intense. I was never free of the critical speech that surrounded me, so self-loathing became part of the everyday thinking process.

I remember wanting to tell a friend of mine about myself. He and I had grown close, and I had great reason to trust him. Then one day at lunch, he told a joke that stopped me in my tracks. "How did the Statue of Liberty get AIDS?" he asked. "From all the fairies passing by!" His laughter let me know that my continued silence was a must.

I was tempted to date girls in middle and high school. My reasoning was twofold. First, I could throw everyone off track from their growing suspicions of my sexuality. Second, with any luck I would be converted. However, intrinsically I knew that I would be using someone for my own selfish gain. The morals of my community and my church environment prevented me from doing that. Anytime I came close to asking a girl out, my fondness for her would not allow me to place her in an unfair position, resulting in more reasons I was unworthy of being around people. I just could not be "normal."

It wasn't until I left that town that I realized how much shame I dealt with growing up. Self-loathing was so natural and so much a part of my identity that I didn't recognize a day without that mindset. I truly didn't know how it felt to face a day without the self-hatred imposed by the shame I grew up with all my life.

The metamorphosis I experienced had its share of casualties. One of them became attendance in church. My belief and faith in God does not dismiss the discomfort I feel when I sense, or am directly told, that someone is trying (very hard) to figure out how I could possibly be a Christian and gay. The moral and Bible battles become overly daunting. Despite my comfort with God's word, it is nearly impossible for me to have a conversation with someone who would prefer I go to hell rather than break bread with me. (Yes, that has been said.) My resolve is to commune with my Lord away from the masses. My prayers are said daily but in private. I still hesitate to tell anyone about my sexuality because other people's predispositions too often have prevented me from feeling safe to be myself. I discuss my sexuality openly, but only with people I have already met and know to be safe. As much as I have rid myself of the old style of thinking, I'm still careful about uncharted territory with people I don't know. People's judgment can be so severe that I have even chosen to publish this essay anonymously.

It took more than 20 years after leaving home before I could wake up and feel comfortable within my own skin. The process was painful, and it required much reflection and forgiveness for both others and myself. I had to reinvent myself, and the learning curve was not in any self-help book I could find. Toxic thoughts still visit sometimes, and I have learned to process through them when needed. I don't know if it is possible to remove oneself totally from the influences under which one grew up. What is true for me is that there were many years of emotional torture I experienced growing up, and again as an adult, while I worked at ridding my mind of those very same demons. Shame is a powerful and all-consuming mindset. It can be overcome, but not without the kind of self-reflection that calls for indescribable anxiety throughout the process.

Comments and actions that can increase shame:

1. Gay jokes or derogatory statements, in particular if there is disloyalty when the person in question is absent. How we speak about others behind their backs tells observers who they can trust and who they cannot.

2. Avoiding stories about people who are homosexual. It comes across as if the topic is too terrible to allow in conversation. The implication is that if the topic is terrible, so are the people.

3. Lowering one's volume or tone when the topic surfaces. Keeping one's rhythm and cadence unsteady throughout a conversation is a cue that there is reason for discomfort.

Comments and actions that promote inner strength:

1. Speaking in the "us" and "we" when discussing communities as a whole.

2. Speaking about those who are absent in a way that preserves their dignity conveys that you are safe when students are both in and out of your presence.

3. Identifying that not every lifestyle needs to be understood by authority figures. There just needs to be respect.

Minority in a predominantly white school: Racial discrimination
by Rickey Frierson, Quantitative Research Associate

Devaughn grew up in a neighborhood that was riddled with crime and had a strong influence of gang culture. Many of the students at his school were conditioned to the reality of being in a single-parent home or having loved ones killed due to gang violence. In fact, Devaughn's own father was gunned down earlier in Devaughn's childhood due to gang violence, and his older brother is currently serving Year 9 of a 15-year sentence.

Devaughn is now the oldest son living with his mother and two younger sisters. In an attempt not to repeat the fate of her other child, the mother decides to move the family across the country to start anew. Devaughn is now in a predominantly rural setting where he is one of a few minority students in his new school.

Devaughn is asked to write a paper about his family and perspective on life. Devaughn writes about his upbringing, previous school, and current family dynamics. Upon reading the teacher's feedback, Devaughn grows upset with her remarks. Devaughn is told that his paper is well written but that he should consider talking to someone about his past and his family encounters.

Devaughn automatically becomes defensive for a few reasons: First, Devaughn never asked for the teacher's comments about his life; he was simply fulfilling the assignment's requirements. Second, her response clearly shows him that she doesn't understand reality outside of her own current environment. Never would a teacher at his previous school consider such a thing because the issues he was writing about are part of everyday life.

Devaughn becomes distant to his new teacher because it's clear she doesn't understand. Therefore, Devaughn is now viewed by the teacher as reluctant for his lack of participation.

To avoid situations that make a person feel less than and separate from, understand the emotional challenges of going to a new city or state and adjusting to something completely new. Try to be understanding when students become defensive or when there are miscommunications. Take into account the emotional detachment of being in a new community where none of your memories were formed. Have patience as students attempt to make friends with people who do not have the same understanding, outlook, or reactions to situations.

Comments that may increase shame:

1. Denying or dismissing the reality of the experience that the student brings to the classroom because the person making the comment has no experience with that reality: "Your experiences are not authentic."

2. Assumption of a person's feelings: "You must be angry inside."

3. Questioning of ability: "You write so well for someone from a bad neighborhood."

4. Assigning causal explanations to behavior without knowing the student: "You are distant because you don't like your new school."

5. Giving unsolicited advice: "You should seek counseling."

Comments that may develop a strong inner self:

1. Identify the strengths that individuals bring with them: "You have many strengths. Which ones will help you with this transition?"

2. Offer support: "Because this place is different than your previous experience, what can I do to make the transition easier?"

3. Seek information: "What would you like me to know about you so that I can make this new school easier/better for you?"

Dual-language, one choice: Dealing with dual-language discrimination

by Ruben Perez, Behavioral Skills Specialist and Independent Consultant

Being a Mexican American who grew up in a border town meant that I grew up in a somewhat monochromatic environment. Ninety-nine percent of the people I grew up with were also Mexican American. Consequently, I grew up in a town that felt like an annexation of Mexico. Spanish was the primary language of the city. Businesses and even street signs were in Spanish most times. The knowledge that I was an American citizen came with an extreme awareness of my Mexican roots as the bigger element that defined all of us as a community and a people.

The conflict with the two cultures coming together came primarily from the influence of school and television. While I was with family and friends, there was great comfort and pride in our common heritage. I am told that I spoke only Spanish before I entered school. I think I did not speak a word of English until the age of five.

All that changed when I started school. The educational system was struggling with a Spanish-speaking community and decided to be very punitive in its attempts to get students to speak English. In elementary school I was punished whenever I was caught speaking Spanish. I remember being denied recess, being made to sit in the corner, and being called out loudly by the teacher in a very authoritarian manner whenever I spoke the forbidden language.

Additionally, Hispanics were never portrayed as intelligent or as independent thinkers on television. I was well aware that anyone who looked like me was always portrayed as servile, submissive, and unintelligent. The unfortunate belief system I adopted was that being Hispanic and speaking Spanish was for second-class citizens, and I had best not act or speak like a Mexican. Consequently, when I learned English somewhere between the ages of five and six, I never spoke Spanish again until the age of 19. By then my Spanish was so bad I didn't speak it much for fear of being ridiculed.

Because there was such a divide in social norms and politics between the two cultures, I somehow learned that I had to choose to be one or the other. Being a Mexican American at the time also meant that I had choose to identify as one or the other: a Mexican or an American. I could not be both. I could either speak Spanish and fit the mold of the Mexican stereotype, or I could speak English and fit the mold of a white wannabe stereotype. My understanding limited me to those two choices.

Despite the fact that I no longer spoke Spanish, I did understand it. When someone spoke to me in Spanish, I replied in English. It was the best compromise I could come up with. It seemed to be a daily battle, and settling for the best of both worlds was an impossible option. As my English improved, I would be accused of being a "coconut" by family and friends. A coconut is someone who is "brown on the outside and white on the inside." Even my father accused me of it.

I learned to hide my intelligence and hold back if I wanted to fit in with other people of my background. (Try doing that while not speaking the language. Very tricky!) However, my desire to become a reporter made language a battleground. I had to improve my English in order to succeed in college. My compromise was to mimic characters on television who were highly intelligent. I would repeat their lines to myself when I was alone.

I will never forget my first day in college away from my hometown. I walked into a classroom that seemed to be filled with an ocean of blonde hair. The visual gave me pause at the door. I felt like I didn't belong, as it was the first time I had ever seen a great number of people who did not look like me.

I took a seat behind a gentleman who acted like the welcome wagon of the classroom. He was joyful and boisterous. He called many classmates by name and asked how they were doing. I imagined they all went to high school together. Then the moment came when he turned around and looked at me.

He paused and continued to smile, but instead of greeting me like he did everyone else, he exuberantly said, *"¿Hola, que tal?"* with a robust, cheerful, and very white accent.

I was frozen in my tracks. I could only stare at him. Within a nanosecond the following questions all raced through my head:

- Why did he talk to me in Spanish?
- Does he think I don't know how to speak English?
- Is he trying to make fun of me in front of everybody else?
- Is he trying to make me feel welcome and putting effort into greeting me in a language he thinks I am comfortable with?
- Does he think I am unintelligent and lazy like the Hispanic stereotypes in the media?
- Should I respond in English?
- Should I respond in Spanish?
- In which language should I answer so as not to come across as arrogant or stupid?

The tsunami of questions that raced through my head caused me to give a very stoic and cold reply. "I'm fine. How are you?"

I can still picture his face. He was just as frozen as I was. I truly did not know what was an appropriate response. Even though I have complete faith that he had every good intention to greet me with kindness, I came to realize that I had a level of shame for my culture because of how it was viewed by the masses. I had shame for what I thought others thought of me.

Time also revealed that I was the one who had to step out of my comfort zone and get to know non-Hispanics for the shame to lift. It is not an exaggeration to say that I could feel myself perspire when I attempted to socialize outside my circle. Feeling as if my physical presence compelled others to think that I was less intelligent and socially less worthy of their company put the responsibility of breaking the thinking pattern on me. It was not easy to feel shame and proceed through introductions and socializing.

Later, when I became an educator, it saddened me to find out that despite all the progress we have made, many students who come from dual-culture backgrounds feel the same way today. There is oftentimes a stigma that comes from stereotypes in the media as to how we are viewed, and more importantly, how we view ourselves.

Consequently, it became my life's mission to help students use their voice in order to find their voice. I've had a great number of students confess to me their level of embarrassment, shame, or fear about not being white. It is a mindset I am all too familiar with still. The only solution I know of is to find all the reasons to be proud of one's own heritage in order to appreciate someone else's.

As we discover the beauty of our own history, it somehow unlocks the mind and heart to feel an intense belonging with all other cultures. Shame prevents pride in self, interaction with others, and a feeling that one has a right to fit into other social circles. It becomes who you are as opposed to who you can become.

Statements and actions that can promote shame:

1. Correcting or chastising someone for not being enough of an example of their heritage or citizenship, e.g., "You're acting too white."

2. Scolding someone for not speaking the language of their heritage.

3. Acting on preconceived notions or stereotypes according to someone's appearance, dialect, vocabulary, grammar, or country of origin, e.g., "Are you Mexican? You sure look like it!"

4. Making fun of someone who does not speak the language of the dominant culture well.

Statements and actions that promote inner strength:

1. Allowing yourself to learn from individuals how they view their own identity, e.g., "What is your country of origin? What do you like best about it? What do you miss most about it?"

2. Acknowledging strengths in both heritage and citizenship.

3. Demonstrating confidence in your own background without it diminishing someone else's.

Third school in two years: Dealing with student mobility

by Rickey Frierson, Quantitative Research Associate

Richard is in a military family and moves a lot. In addition to moving, his mother is a high-ranking official in the U.S. Army. Richard is in high school and has a hard time explaining his family dynamics. Although he has both parents, he views a majority of his childhood as growing up in a single-parent house because his mother is always gone.

To many, Richard is viewed as very harsh and crass towards others. However, Richard's home is very structured and orderly. Richard does not view his communication with his fellow students as crass or harsh but just straightforward and honest. Even his teachers sometimes think he is a little disrespectful in how he conveys his thoughts in class. But Richard remembers his mother telling him to be frank. Additionally, Richard has been at so many schools that he has learned not really to be concerned with pleasing the teachers and other students because it's only a matter of time before he and his family move again.

Richard does not have many friends, and after the third school in two years, he figures what is the point of trying to please and attempt to make friends when the hurt follows as soon as he has to move? His mother is gone years at a time, and his father works long hours.

As an only child, Richard has grown accustomed to a life of isolation and thus has decided to be himself and not worry about social interactions or concerning himself with others' feelings. For a large portion of Richard's childhood, he was a latchkey kid. He would be alone in the apartment for 2–3 hours after school until his father got home from work. Richard could not play with kids after school because there was no way for him to get home from the after-school program; therefore, his parents thought it best and safer for him to just have a key to the apartment and stay home until his father returned. Richard could not answer the door for anyone because he was instructed that the only people who should be coming into the home would already have a key.

How does this situation make a person feel 'less than' and 'separate from?'

How does one explain having two parents but living like they're from a single-parent household? Richard, as an only child, may have developed attachment issues in relationships where he does not allow himself to attach fully due to previous experiences of leaving. Thus, the concerns about breakups with emotional attachments may be too much for Richard. Richard also has to battle the stigma that children without siblings are supposed to be spoiled; yet, his experiences as a military child and also as an only child have caused Richard to think the affection in his own childhood was "less than" because he never felt spoiled.

Comments that may increase shame:

1. No understanding of the impact of mobility on a student's motivation to form relationships: "Why don't you like our school? Why don't you have friends?"

2. Assumptions about family structure: "But you have a two-parent household, so what is the problem? You are spoiled because you're an only child."

3. No understanding of how the external environment impacts friendships and relationships: "You are emotionally distant, and that is why you do not have friends."

Comments that may strengthen the inner self:

1. Are there friends you keep up with on social media?

2. What do you like best about your new school? What do you like least?

3. Who do you care the most about? Who cares the most about you? (Listen for adults.)

When you don't like your new family: Foster care

by Rickey Frierson, Quantitative Research Associate

Gavin has been in the foster care system since he was eight due to his mother's drug issues and his absent father. Gavin has been in more than 12 homes due to disruption and violence. Teachers have noticed that his attitudes and behaviors worsen from October to January.

It was discovered that Gavin's behavior worsens when nearing the major holidays with family, but that was also around the time Gavin was placed in the foster care system. Gavin doesn't like going to school and talking about what other kids are doing with their families because Gavin hasn't been able to spend time with his biological family or siblings. Gavin grows increasingly frustrated about having to sit in class activities in which they talk about things to be thankful for and plans for family vacation.

Gavin doesn't like his foster family. They don't know him, but they expect him to just obey all their rules. Some of the family's customs are foreign to Gavin and do not make sense. In some cases, his foster families say things are okay to do that his biological parents told him were wrong. He is torn and confused about what rules to follow. He fears that if he just does what all the other families ask, then he will disappoint his biological parents when he is reunited with them.

How does this situation make a person feel 'less than' and 'separate from?'

In foster situations there is often emotional allegiance and hope that one day you will be reunited with your biological family. Gavin may be feeling that if he continues to disrupt and cause issues, then they will work harder to have him reunited with his biological family.

Foster families have good intentions to provide a safe space for Gavin but may not realize that Gavin feels isolated the entire time. Gavin's family never gave him away; rather, he was taken away from his family. But the foster family just gave up on him, and so he doesn't feel loved and appreciated like they want him to.

Comments that may create shame:

1. You should be so happy that you are away from your bad parents.
2. You should be happy and grateful to have a family that is taking care of you.
3. This year you will have fabulous holidays.
4. How many families have you been with? You must be a problem.

Comments that may help develop a strong inner self:

1. As you have watched many adults, what behaviors do adults use that benefit you?
2. What is the hardest part of the holidays? Are there any aspects of the holidays that you like?

Don't you want to put some makeup on? Dealing with gender and body discrimination

by Dr. Haley Ford, Community Engagement Specialist

The first time I felt shame attached to my body and to my gender, I was 10 years old. The summer after fifth grade, I went to the community pool with one of my friends. After our fingers were appropriately pruney, we wrapped our damp towels around our bodies and trotted back towards my house. As we rounded a corner, coming towards us was a pair of boys about our same age, clearly headed in the direction we had just come from.

I thought nothing of it, but as soon as they were close enough, "SLAP!" I felt a hand strike my buttock. By the time I was able to comprehend what had happened, I turned and they were gone. I could only barely hear a giggle as they ran into the distance. I tried my best not to cry until I walked through my back door.

I told my very Southern father what had transpired with tears restricted just enough to blur my vision but never spill over. He became quiet. He slowly bent down, got nose to nose with me, and said, "If you ever see those boys again, you beat the tar out of 'em."

Two life-altering realizations took place that day. First, after having been introduced to the idea that belonging to the female gender held different meaning than identifying as "boy" or "male," I recognized that ownership of my body seemed to be up for debate. Lastly, when I expected my father to react to this violation by getting into his truck to find those boys and "defend my honor," he chose a path of empowerment. He chose to give back to me my autonomy. He chose to see my strengths and gift me the chance to defend my own honor because he knew I was capable of that task.

Something about who I thought I was shifted that day.

While growing up, I continued to have experiences that shamed me in connection to my gender. As I went through puberty in adolescence, I physically developed early, and by the time I turned 12, I had the body of an adult woman. This caused my clothes to seemingly shrink overnight. I went to school in a sweater that I wore all too frequently, but I would never wear the sweater again after this particular day.

As I was talking with my friends in the hallway before class, the assistant principal strode up to me, walkie-talkie and unwavering authority in hand. She sternly pointed at my chest, and in front of 10 other 15-year-olds demanded, "You need to zip that sweater up, or you'll be sent home."

I am sure my face went beet red instantaneously. I tried as quickly as I could to zip up the sweater, but when I attempted to pull the tab up to my collarbone, I could barely breathe. I had not realized the sweater did not fit anymore. I wanted to hide. I spent the rest of the school day frequently going to bathroom so that I could unzip the sweater and breathe normally for a short while. I made sure to check how my clothes fit from that point on.

Throughout my entire schooling experience, I have existed outside of the expectations of my gender, and it has caused me to endure many wounds. Another event that left a scar was from the summer I went to visit the college of my choice. Since it was Texas and more than 100 degrees outside, I chose to wear my favorite baseball cap with no makeup.

As I was tying my long hair up into the back of the cap, my mother said, "Don't you want to put some makeup on?"

I was shocked and embarrassed. I felt the shame rise up in my chest, and I pulled my cap low over my eyes. I never thought my mother would see my face as "less than," and in my pain, I responded with anger and resentment. We did not speak for the remainder of the day. Something had broken between my mother and me.

It seemed that every time I tried to be comfortable in my own skin, I was shamed into another box, eventually teaching me what it meant to be the "right kind of woman."

After many years of being called horrible names and having those derogatory names reinforced by family, teachers, and friends, I am finally comfortable with the fact that I love who I am and the skin I am in. I would not describe myself as a gender revolutionary, gender creative, or even gender nonconforming, only as someone who knows what it feels like when society says, "Get back in line!" I only want to play my contact sports and wear my lipstick too.

If a student falls outside the gender binary, these kinds of comments may increase shame:

1. Ignoring capabilities and strengths: "I need three strong boys to help me lift these boxes."

2. Belittling identities: "Don't be such a girl!" "Man up!" "Boys don't cry!"

3. Assigning value or worth to appearance: "Why is it that you never wear makeup to school? You would be so much prettier with it on!"

4. Assuming anything based on gender or appearances: "Wow! You play a boy's sport?! That's really surprising."

Comments and actions that promote inner strength:

1. Acknowledging and promoting capabilities and strengths: "Can I have three volunteers to help me lift this?"

2. Empowering identity: "You are entitled to your feelings." "You are smart and capable."

3. Seeing value in skills and knowledge: "You are so talented, and you work so hard."

4. Embracing the value of diversity: "You and your story are worthy and important."

'Less than' and 'separate from' online: Dealing with bullying in the age of social media

In the research on bullying, students who bully are neither at the top of the social status ladder or the bottom. Rather, they are in the middle, working to climb the social status ladder.[56] Bullying almost always comes out of a weak inner self and is motivated by envy, the need to control, and the need to be socially included (particularly for females) or to exclude someone. Interestingly, in the gender research, females have many friends if they bully and likely bully people they know. Males have few friends if they bully and most likely don't know the people they bully very well.

Because bullying seems to be linked to social status, it is interesting to note that females tend to believe that social hierarchies will destroy friendships. Males tend to believe that social hierarchies will build friendships.

The use of social media has increased bullying among adolescents. The research indicates that the greater the amount of time an adolescent spends engaged in social media, the greater the likelihood the adolescent will suffer from increased unhappiness and depression.

Internet and social media bullying

One of the more painful experiences of my professional life has been the amount of Internet and social media bullying that has occurred around me personally and the work on financial poverty (*A Framework for Understanding Poverty*). One critic said in public that it was his goal to "destroy Ruby Payne and her work." One workshop participant told me, "You have no right to talk about poverty. You are white. Poverty belongs to minorities." I have been labeled as "racist" because I did not talk about race and poverty together. It is bullying the person.

There has been a great deal of bullying at the professional level. A major educational journal published a very critical article about the work, gave me 24 hours to write a response, and limited my response to 25% of the words of the original article. When I asked to be able to write a full article with appropriate details and information for a later publication, the answer was, "No, you cannot." In other words, "We will participate in the bullying, and you will not have a voice." Organizations have been called by my critics and told that if they bring me in to speak or consult, the critics will go to the media and say that the hosting organization is racist.

Professional bullying is often about ideology, envy, and professional gain. At a conference, a nontenured professor was critiquing *Framework*. A friend of mine was in the audience. She went up to him afterward and said, "Ruby does not say what you said she says."

He said to her, "I don't care what she says. If I use her name in a paper as a critical review, I get it accepted, and I can count that paper toward tenure."

Bullying impugns identity (who you are). If the bullying has to do with your skin color or your body or your attributes, there is little that can be done about that.

The worst part about being bullied on the Internet is:

1. You cannot be seen or heard for who you are.
2. It is hard to fight back. (Who do you hit?)
3. You have no control over the size of the audience. Many people make a decision about you without knowing anything about you.
4. It results in personal or professional exclusion.

Internet bullying involves the following: Pick out a detail or aspect of a person or idea, distort and enlarge that particular detail, omit key information, and "smear" the professional or personal reputation of the individual. Often the supporters of the person being bullied will also be targeted. The result is that people stay clear of you simply because of the confusion, the amount of time it takes to figure out the actual truth, and the fear of being smeared themselves with the same brush.

One of the ways you know that the bullying is a coordinated effort on the part of more than one person is that the same words and phrases show up again and again. In *The Smear,* Sharyl Attkisson identifies this characteristic in organized Internet smearing. Usually there are four or five key words or terms that constantly show up.[57] In my case, the words and terms were *deficit model, stereotyping, racist, not research-based,* and *culture of poverty.*

Bullying works best when the words used are simple, easy to repeat, and negative in connotation.

For adolescents, Internet and social media bullying is almost always personal. The gain for those who bully is social status and control. Because adolescence is a time when identity and peer acceptance is so critical for adult development, this bullying can be devastating.

There is a tendency on the part of adults to dismiss Internet and social media bullying of adolescents as unimportant. Adults who do that have never personally experienced the rage, frustration, discouragement, helplessness, and anger at the incredible emotional impact of such activity.

How did I deal with it? I wrote an article as a response to the critics.[58] But I also realized the following: (a) It did not change my future story or take away what I love to do—which is understand how people learn and know what they know, (b) for every professional exclusion ("don't come because we don't want to deal with the noise"), there were 4–5 people who said, "We don't care about the criticism. The information works, and we want to use it," and (c) it did not affect my close friendships.

I was in my 50s when this Internet bullying started. I had a strong sense of self and had many professional successes. I cannot imagine what it must be like to be in your teens and have this happen to you when you are trying to figure out who you are. *The experience of being bullied is not to be underestimated.*

Comments or actions that may increase shame:

1. You should not let that bother you.

2. Sticks and stones may break my bones, but words alone cannot.

3. Why are you crying about that? You should be tougher.

4. Refusing to discuss the issue or being dismissive of the issue.

5. What did you do to make them say that?

Comments or actions that may increase inner strength:

1. Are the comments actually true? Can you identify times when those comments are false?

2. What is the motivation behind the bullying? Envy? Control? Social exclusion/inclusion? Personal gain?

3. Tell me about your good, solid friends who support you.

4. Will this bullying affect your future story? Can it take away what you love to do?

5. In five years, will these comments make a difference in your life?

Resentment

According to Jordan Peterson, a clinical psychologist, "there are only two major reasons for resentment: being taken advantage of (or allowing yourself to be taken advantage of), or whiny refusal to adopt responsibility and grow up."[59]

Resentment often occurs in the context of fairness or unmerited advantage. Every human being at one time or another has lamented and resented a situation because of unfairness or unmerited advantage. Resentment is very common when a child is required to take on adult responsibilities because of a parent who works two jobs, a parent who has an addiction, a parent who has a physical/mental illness, etc.

In the school business, unfairness often gets confused in the conversation between equity and equality. When students complained about things being unfair, I explained it this way: If the students wore glasses, I would tell the students to take them off and not use them. (If the students did not wear glasses, I would tell them to find a pair and wear them). The students would protest that they did or did not need the glasses. Then I would say this: "Every human being has strengths and liabilities. The issue is to make the playing field as level as possible—while understanding that not everyone is the same." I would stress that opportunity should be equal, but adaptations would always be necessary.

True resentment occurs when the needs of the individual are negated to meet the needs of someone else. True resentment almost always involves a power issue.

The demands of survival often create resentments.

Rage, revenge, and violence

Rage often comes out of contempt. Violence comes from too little compassion.

> *The problem of violence is less a matter of too much of something* (e.g., anger, aggression, exertion of power and control, negative attitudes toward women and children) *than of too little of something, namely compassion, moral judgement and relationship skills* ... Research indicates that merely changing situational behavior runs the risk of increasing physical abuse ... or increasing psychological abuse even as physical abuse wanes ... Social attitudes are the most superficial facet of an individual's belief system. They reflect self-constructions while having no causal effect on them. As such they serve merely as excuses.[60]

According to Salman Akhtar and Henri Parens in their book *Revenge: Narcissistic Injury, Rage, and Retaliation,* revenge involves rage, envy, and resentment.

> An injury that has been repaid, even if only in words, is recollected quite differently from one that has to be accepted ... an injury that has been suffered in silence as "a mortification" ... The injured person's reaction to the trauma only exercises a completely "cathartic" effect if it is an adequate reaction—as, for instance, revenge.[61]

Akhtar and Parens go on to say that using language to explore the damage rather than taking an action is almost as effective.

In the research, compassion, kindness, gratitude, and reparation act as a counterbalance to malignant narcissism and revenge. However, the researchers noted that often individuals who have malignant narcissism and envy hate goodness, kindness, and support. The reason is that without the anger and rage, the self-soothing that occurs is absent, and the weak inner self is not soothed.

What does this mean in your classroom?

1. First of all, if you take the behavior personally, you have missed the point. *It is not about you.* It is an attempt to address a weak inner self on the part of the individual with whom you are dealing.

2. It is important to know what the motivators and payoffs are for anger, resentment, rage, avoidance, and anxiety. Each of these behaviors is perceived by the student as providing an advantage so that the emotional reality can be survived.

What does this mean for your campus?

1. *Triage those students who are most at risk for anger, revenge, and violence.* Schools know who these students are when they are quite young.

2. In the past we have kicked out students whose behavior cannot be contained at school. We have not provided an avenue or transition for more help and support for those individuals. There is nothing to keep them from coming back and killing—except for security, which can be limited. Schools know by the third grade who the truly troubled students are. Interventions and referrals to the larger behavioral healthcare community need to be made at that time.

Process of emotional triage to increase school safety

1. Gather a team of individuals at your campus to include principal, assistant principal, counselor(s), social workers, psychologist, nurse, et al.

2. Have each teacher submit a list of the students who have the most anger, anxiety, violent tendencies, social isolation, or who display other difficult behavior.

3. As a team, assign each student on the list to a group.

Insecure, anxious-avoidant (social isolates)	Insecure, anxious-ambivalent	Disorganized/dismissive (safe and dangerous)

4. For each group, identify the top 50% who are most unstable in terms of behavior and emotional response.

5. Make a school safety plan for each student in the top 50%. What will be done consistently with each student? Include the following:

a. Who will talk to each student every day for 3–4 minutes one-on-one?

b. Who will monitor the emotional stability of each student?

c. What is the protocol for referral systems for safe and dangerous students? If they must be removed from the school, what is done to make sure that they are not further shamed, isolated, and seeking revenge? (The young man who killed 17 individuals at Marjory Stoneman Douglas High School in Florida had his father die in 2004, and his mother died three months before the shooting. He was kicked out of high school for his behavior, and in rage, shame, and anger, he killed. When he got kicked out, he was referred to an intervention program but didn't complete it. More effort should have been put forth to ensure he got the interventions he needed—and that he followed through with those interventions.)

Gender Issues

Why do I have so many discipline referrals for males? Why do they shut down and quit?

There are gender differences in emotional processing and need. Why is this important to know?

Every child should have equal opportunity to develop talents, to live, to love, to work, to learn.

However, no two children are alike. I ask parents, "How would it work if you treated all of your children the same and expected exactly the same out of each child?"

Every parent I ask simply laughs and says, "Not possible."

The gender issue in general is very complicated, but the U.S. has a particular problem: 85% of educators in K–12 are female, but roughly 50% of the student population is male. Couple this with the fact that the majority of discipline referrals, nonreaders, special education students, and dropouts are male, and you see that the numbers do not work. At the college level, 65% of college graduates are now female.

It is clear that we are not educating male students well. Schools are not preparing males for postsecondary education, and they are not preparing them to enter the workforce.

A word of caution: Gender difference is a political hot topic.

There is perhaps no greater disparity than to treat all differences as the same—the equal treatment of differences. When I hear an educator say, "I treat all of my students the same," I know they are not a very good educator. First of all, it is not possible, and secondly, it is not desirable. Many of the gifts of humanity are our differences and diversity.

Like I said, proceed with caution: Gender differences are complicated and politically sensitive topics.

"To say the least it [the debate over brain differences] is a fairly passionate and politicized one. On the one hand are people who claim that hardwired male/female brain differences can explain all sorts of behavioral differences—that women simply are, on average, more nurturing, while men are more aggressive. On the other are those who claim that there's really no such thing as a 'male' or a 'female' brain, and that these distinctions have been used to support sexist beliefs and policies."[62]

"Scientists generally study four primary areas of difference in male and female brains: processing, chemistry, structure, and activity. These differences between male and female brains in these areas show up all over the world, but scientists also have discovered exceptions to every so-called gender rule."[63]

In a study at the University of Edinburgh, Scotland, a group of 18 researchers looked at data from more than 5,000 people who agreed to scan their brains as part of the UK Biobank. It is the biggest single study of sex differences in the human brain. They found the following:

1. There are differences between male and female brains. There is also a lot of overlap.

2. These differences could help better understand diseases that impact one sex more than another.

3. The study had no causal conclusions (nurture versus nature).[64]

A second analysis of the data found that "brain features correctly predicted subjects' sex about 69–77% of the time."[65]

In processing, male brains use about seven times more gray matter for activity than female brains do. Gray matter areas are information- and action-processing centers. This gray matter allows for more focused activity. Female brains use nearly 10 times more white matter. White matter connects the gray matter and other processing centers with one another. This allows for more networking and multitasking.[66]

Structurally, male and female brains tend to have different hemispheric divisions of labor. Females process language on both sides of the brain. Males tend to use only the left hemisphere for language. Furthermore, there is less connectivity in male brains between their word centers and their memories and feelings. The hippocampus in a female brain tends to be larger and tends to have a higher density of neural connections. Therefore, female brains tend to take in more sensory data about their surroundings and remember it more vividly. Male brains have a larger amygdala than female brains, even after the difference in overall brain size is accounted for. (Males tend to have larger brains in part because they tend to have larger bodies.)

Emotional processing for females tends to occur faster because of more blood flow between the right and left brain. Male brains take longer to process emotions.

Chemically, both brains process serotonin (calming and feeling good), testosterone (sex and aggression), estrogen (female growth and reproduction), and oxytocin (bonding and relationships). These chemicals tend to be processed differently. "Males on average tend to be less inclined to sit still for as long as females and tend to be more physically impulsive and aggressive. Additionally, males process less of the bonding chemical oxytocin than females."[67]

Do boys and girls learn differently? Does "nature" or "nurture" have a more profound impact on learning and emotional processing? The answer to both questions is yes. Boys and girls can obtain the same level of education, but the means by which they reach the same level may be different.

The concept of gender has become a pressing issue today. Is gender determined by sex assignment at birth? Are males those with XY chromosomes and females those with XX chromosomes (nature), or is gender determined by social/cultural norms (nurture)? Researchers are constantly examining and interpreting their findings, and they don't always agree. One of the main problems with the research is that the samples are small and subject to political interpretation. If you apply the research findings to only one sex or the other, someone will always find the exception and claim the research is flawed or biased.

There are a number of patterns or tendencies that can be found that show some similarities and differences between males and females. These patterns can have a major impact on students' learning and their ability to deal with emotional problems. One tendency or pattern is not better than another, nor is one right and the other wrong. There are always exceptions to these patterns, and it would be absolutely wrong to assume that these patterns are absolutes. Assuming that the patterns are absolutes is what leads to bias and stereotyping. Boys and girls can do the same things; they may just do them differently.

Female/male tendencies or patterns

Tendency/ pattern	Females tend to	Males tend to
Maturity	Complete brain growth earlier	Complete brain growth later[68]
Memory	Retain sensory memory with great detail	Not retain sensory memory with great detail[69]
Processing information	Process information between and across both hemispheres	Process information back and forth within hemispheres[70]
Brain at rest	Continue to have activity throughout the brain when they are in the rest state	Have limited brain activity when they are in the rest state[71]
Focus	Stay focused for longer periods of time without the need for movement	Stay focused longer when movement is part of learning[72]
Focus	Focus on faces and things	Focus on movement[73]
Focus	Make transitions more quickly and can multitask	Transition more slowly and will focus on one task at a time[74]
Focus	Want to face others when communicating, be smiled at	Avoid eye contact, prefer you sit beside them[75]
Spatial awareness	Be better at object discrimination (what is it?)	Be better at object location (where is it?)[76]
Directionality	Use landmarks to give directions	Use compass points to give directions[77]
Fine motor skills	Develop fine motor skills earlier	Take longer to develop fine motor skills[78]

(continued on next page)

(continued from previous page)

Tendency/ pattern	Females tend to	Males tend to
Gross motor skills	Take longer to develop gross motor skills	Develop gross motor skills earlier[79]
Hearing	Have better hearing and are distracted by loud noise	Lose attention if they cannot hear[80]
Emotions	Have more serotonin and oxytocin	Have less serotonin and oxytocin[81]
Emotions	Explain and describe their emotions with detail	Find it difficult to explain their emotions[82]
Emotions	Not deal with moderate stress successfully	Deal with moderate stress more successfully; may find it a challenge to take on[83]
Emotions	Feel uncomfortable when faced with confrontation	Feel excited when faced with confrontation[84]
Aggressive play	Not engage in aggressive play	Engage in aggressive play often[85]
Self-esteem	Underestimate their skills and look for support on challenging tasks	Overestimate their skills and prefer to solve challenging tasks alone[86]
Self-esteem	Need encouragement to build success	Need reality checks to effectively assess abilities and limitations[87]
Self-esteem	Often ask for help to accomplish tasks	Not ask for help to avoid being perceived as "dumb"[88]
Friendships	Be focused on other girls	Be focused on shared activities or likes[89]
Friendships	View conversation as essential to the friendship	View conversation as not essential[90]
Friendships	Believe that social hierarchies will destroy friendships	Believe that social hierarchies will build friendships[91]
Friendships	Believe that self-revelation and sharing are important	Believe that self-revelation should be avoided[92]
Friendships	Want to be with friends when under stress	Want to be alone when facing stressful situations[93]
Friendships	Have many friends if they bully, and likely bully someone they know	Have few friends if they bully, and most likely don't know the person they bully very well[94]

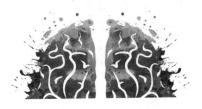

Part of the conversation about males is this dilemma:

How does a male become "tough enough" to handle the reality of the working world of men, yet maintain his ability to address his own emotional issues?

According to clinical psychologist Jordan Peterson,

> men have to toughen up … If you think tough men are dangerous, wait until you see what weak men are capable of … Men toughen up by pushing themselves and by pushing each other … by doing dangerous things, trying to make themselves useful. When this process goes too far, boys drift into antisocial behavior, which is far more prevalent in males.[95]

One of the key factors is whether or not a male has the language for feelings, the recognition of those feelings, and the tools to deal with those feelings. The second key factor is whether or not he has had an adult male role model.

I worked with a group of homeless men on my book with Emilia O'Neill-Baker, *How Much of Yourself Do You Own?* I said I wanted to work with a group of men because it seemed that feelings were addressed less with males than with females. One of the men said to me, "We got feelings! We just don't know what to do with them!"

What does this mean in the classroom?

1. Give male brains more processing time for emotional issues. When stressed, male brains prefer to be silent. When a male brain takes an emotional "hit"—anything that jeopardizes safety or belonging—it takes much longer to process the emotional significance of that "hit." Some research indicates it takes 3–5 hours of processing time. Female brains tend to process emotion much faster—literally in minutes. The first female response is typically to cry and talk. In schools, when two males get in a fight and are brought in to a female teacher or administrator, typically the first demand is for the male students to talk. When they do not talk immediately and tell the authority figures what happened, then the male students are often punished a second time for "recalcitrance and disrespect." If a female student gets in a fight and cries and talks, she is not punished a second time for that. But we punish males a second time for not talking, or we berate them and chastise them for not talking.

2. Males prefer a shoulder-to-shoulder conversation when there is an emotional issue, rather than an eye-to-eye conversation. Sit beside males, not across from them, and avoid eye contact if you want them to open up.

3. Males will talk more if they can do something with their hands while they talk. For example, if I want my son to talk to me, I will ask him if he will cook with me.

Follow the bouncing ball

Ruben Perez, a friend of mine who shared a story earlier in the book, was a behavioral specialist in a school in the Houston area. Two fifth-grade boys got in a fight. The female principal called the boys in, and for 45 minutes she tried to get them to tell her what happened. They would not talk. She said to Ruben, "They are yours. See if you can find out what happened."

Ruben gave each boy a bottle of water to drink. He sat one boy outside his door and the other in his office. Ruben and the first boy were sitting shoulder to shoulder. The boy was about three feet away. While the boy was drinking the water, Ruben did not speak to the boy, but instead started bouncing a tennis ball. The boy started watching the tennis ball. (Male retinas are hardwired to follow movement. Female retinas are hardwired to see detail and color.)

When the boy was finished drinking the water, Ruben said to him, "I am going to bounce the ball to you, and then you bounce it back to me."

Ruben did this about three or four times and then said to the boy, "So, what happened?" Within five minutes Ruben had the whole story. It is not that the boy was recalcitrant or uncooperative. He was simply processing in his own way.

Additional issues

1. Because female retinas take in more light than male retinas, seeing detail and color is often easier for females. This starts very early and can be seen in pre-K and kindergarten. The teacher asks the students to color a picture, and the girls will often have the correct colors within the lines. Males will often pick up the crayons and scribble. It's about movement. Detail and color also can assist a person in being more organized with paper, etc.

2. When males get stressed, they will often shut down and refuse to work. Remember that males are shame-phobic. If there is an assignment that a male thinks he might not be able to do, he will simply refuse and shut down. Getting the student to move, assigning him work with another student, or making the activity relational (as part of a group) and/or competitive will help the student start working.

3. Male brains can be more compartmentalized than female brains. They use more gray matter and less white matter. Males may get frustrated if topics are changed quickly and without a signal that the topic is going to change.

4. Male brains tend to hear less than female brains. If a student is having difficulty paying attention, then move the student closer to the teacher's desk.

5. Language is not processed as quickly in male brains as it is in female brains. A male will not necessarily respond with lots of language. If the male is from financial poverty, he will have about half the words in his vocabulary that a male from an educated household will have. Do not expect a detailed explanation of what happened.

6. Provide a page of emoji for all students (male and female) to use as a part of the process of naming emotions.

7. When a male shuts down, three strategies tend to help: movement of any kind (e.g., manufacture an errand to the office); working with a buddy; and making a relational, competitive activity out of an academic task.

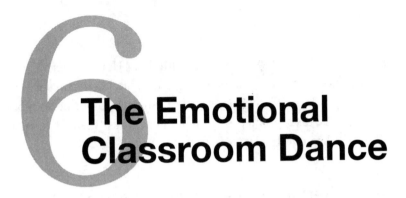

The Emotional
Classroom Dance

Why is there so much emotional
noise in the classroom? Especially
before and after holidays?

So, who just walked into your classroom?

A lot more people than you realize.

Johnny brought his dead father, his angry mother, and his drug-addicted sister with him into the room. They live inside his head and influence his decisions. (Family therapist Virginia Satir indicates that dead people play more of a role in the family than the live ones do.[96])

Marissa brought in her parents' argument from last night (the recent hurricane destroyed the house, but they must pay the mortgage even though the house is gone), her boyfriend who broke up with her because he found out she is living in a tent and no longer gets a shower every day, and the fight she just had with her best friend. She is thinking about suicide.

Juan brought his mother with him because he is terrified that his mother will be deported. She cried last night and talked about what to do if she is not home when he gets home. Where will he go? And will he promise to take care of his baby sister?

Catherine Marie brought her mother with her. Her mother is anxious that Catherine will not be elected homecoming queen, and how can she hold her head up at the country club if Catherine is such a failure? Catherine also brings in her father, who will be disappointed if his daughter is "less than." Catherine takes an Adderall to get through the day.

And then there is you—the educator. You brought people with you too!

You walked into your classroom/campus this morning. You may have brought with you your husband (who just lost his job), your daughter (you are worried she might be pregnant), and your principal/assistant superintendent (who told you that your test scores must improve).

In addition, the bonding and attachment style of the student comes into the room, and the bonding and attachment style of the educator comes in too.

Pick out three students who create a lot of emotional noise for you in your classroom. Who do you think they brought in with them?

Your emotional classroom looks like this:

Lots of emotional noise in the room.

Many times, when students react, it is not you they are reacting to. It is the people they brought into the room with them.

How do you handle this? Are you going to know every student's emotional issues?

No.

Handling this requires that you can:

1. Name the emotional reality
2. Manage the safety and belonging in the classroom
3. Identify the ways in which you, the educator:
   a. Motivate good behavior
   b. Do not cause worse behavior
   c. Develop emotional competence in students

There is an emotional dance that goes on every day in the classroom (and throughout the building) between the educator and the students. It is a dance between safety (control) and belonging, between relationships and structure, or as some would put it, between discipline and learning. This dance is often (but not always) a mirror of the emotional inner hurts and strengths of the educator and of the students. The way in which the dance is conducted is dependent on both the educator's and the students' emotional understandings.

Schools are very good about containing or expelling the bad behaviors, but educators have had very little information on emotional realities and how to motivate good behaviors. To motivate good behaviors, it is important to understand the emotional classroom dance.

Emotions are often triggered by the stimuli of a larger context—in this case, the classroom.

I have worked with each of the individuals in these case studies. They are real people, but their names have been changed to protect identity.

Alecia

Alecia was a first-year fifth-grade teacher. Pretty and tall, she liked students. The discipline in her classroom was problematic. She formed close relationships with her students. In fact, she referred to them as her friends.

One day I got a call from one of the parents who said to me, "Did you know that the fifth-graders are de-pantsing each other?" (This is when students wear sweat suits, and another student will come up from behind and pull the pants down so the student is "mooning" another student.)

I was not aware of this. I went to Alecia and said to her, "Did you know this was happening?"

She said, "Yes."

I said, "How long has this been going on?"

She said, "About a month."

I said, "What have you done about it?"

She said, "I told them it was not nice. That they should not do it."

I said, "You must tell them no. If they do it, there are consequences."

She said, "I cannot do that."

I said, "You cannot tell them no?"

She said, "No, I cannot say no to them. They are my friends."

Alecia never changed her concept of the students being her friends, in spite of my attempts to coach her cognitively. She was dismissed at the end of the year. Her issue was not a cognitive one. She had set up her relationships with students to mirror her emotional understandings of relationships with friends.

Emotional noise

Emotional realities of the teacher

LOW NOISE
- Bonding and attachment style of teacher is secure
- Teacher knows own triggers
- Emotional issues are named accurately
- Discipline and relationships are focused on motivating good behaviors

HIGH NOISE
- Bonding and attachment style is insecure
- Teacher often responds to own emotional triggers
- Discipline motivates more bad behaviors
- Relationships with students are minimal or inappropriate

Emotional realities of the classroom

LOW NOISE
- Classroom management systems are in place
- Discipline is minimal yet effective
- Strategies are in place to motivate good behaviors
- Processes are in place to deal with holidays

HIGH NOISE
- Classroom chaotic and often out of control
- Classroom has favorite students
- Strategies are about survival
- No coherent systems in place

Emotional realities of the 10–15% with the most emotional issues

LOW NOISE
- Students are triaged
- A daily contact is made with each student
- Emotional issues are monitored on a weekly basis

HIGH NOISE
- No triage in place
- These students are ostracized, punished, and bullied
- Teacher reacts to incident when it occurs—no preplanning for response
- Rigidity of approach to students, zero tolerance

Larry

Larry was a sixth-grade teacher of a self-contained classroom. In his mid-40s, he had never been married. He was a key negotiator for the teachers union and was running the campaign of the school board president for her candidacy for the state legislature. He had been moved from building to building because of the difficulties he created—mostly with the staff and administrators. He had put one principal in psychiatric care for 10 years.

When I became the principal, the assistant superintendent told me that there were some "difficult individuals" in the building but did not give any names. Several times the rumor had reached me that Larry would get mad at students and throw them up against the wall. Before school started, I met with him and said, "I am sure this is just a rumor. But rumor has it that you get mad at students and throw them up against the wall." He did not say anything.

I said, "I am sure this is just a rumor. However, you should know that if you do that on my watch, I will do everything in my power to get you dismissed."

One day I was in the sixth-grade hall, and I watched a sixth-grade student we'll call "Milton" do something that we would not let any student do. And Larry was watching Milton do that. I said, "We do not let students do this here." It surprised me that Larry was allowing the behavior to happen because he was usually fairly strict with students.

He said to me, "His dad is a VP of an international company. He won't let Milton have any consequences."

I said, "That is not good for Milton, and it is not good for us. I am going to put him in detention."

Larry laughed and said, "Good luck."

I called Milton's father, discussed it with him, and put Milton in detention with his father's blessing.

One day Larry came to me before school started, very upset, and said to me, "You need to go out to the playground and tell that father that he has to leave."

I said, "Is he doing something wrong?"

Larry said, "He's watching his daughter play on the playground."

I said, "Is he doing something wrong? Bothering anyone else?"

Larry said, "No. I can't stand him. I don't like him. Get him out of here."

I said, "No. He is not harming anyone. He has the right to be there."

Larry said, "You are no kind of a principal. If you were a good principal, you would make him leave."

I said, "That may be that I am no kind of a principal. But I am the principal. And the father will stay."

Emotional noise

Emotional realities of the teacher

LOW NOISE		HIGH NOISE
• Bonding and attachment style of teacher is secure • Teacher knows own triggers • Emotional issues are named accurately • Discipline and relationships are focused on motivating good behaviors	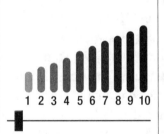	• Bonding and attachment style is insecure • Teacher often responds to own emotional triggers • Discipline motivates more bad behaviors • Relationships with students are minimal or inappropriate

Emotional realities of the classroom

LOW NOISE		HIGH NOISE
• Classroom management systems are in place • Discipline is minimal yet effective • Strategies are in place to motivate good behaviors • Processes are in place to deal with holidays		• Classroom chaotic and often out of control • Classroom has favorite students • Strategies are about survival • No coherent systems in place

Emotional realities of the 10–15% with the most emotional issues

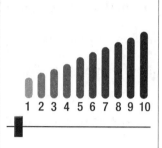

LOW NOISE		HIGH NOISE
• Students are triaged		• No triage in place
• A daily contact is made with each student		• These students are ostracized, punished, and bullied
• Emotional issues are monitored on a weekly basis	1 2 3 4 5 6 7 8 9 10	• Teacher reacts to incident when it occurs—no preplanning for response
		• Rigidity of approach to students, zero tolerance

George

George was a high school English teacher and drama teacher. He was a very seasoned teacher. Nearly six feet tall and very slender, he always had an air of anger and arrogance about him. He viewed his colleagues as mostly plebeians and individuals to be tolerated. His classroom was very structured, and there were no discipline issues. Any infraction and the student was sent out of the classroom or humiliated in front of the other students. He did have a sense of humor, but it was fairly sarcastic. He loved drama in particular and was quite exacting with the students who participated. His failure rate was higher than other teachers. His levels of achievement were also higher than other teachers.

One day I told him that he had to teach ninth-graders and that every teacher in the English department was going to teach one class of ninth-graders. This would ensure that there was a very realistic understanding of our students and would provide the very best teachers at all levels. He said to me, "You are asking me to cast pearls before swine."

I said to him, "Are you a master teacher?"

He said, "Yes."

I said, "It is actually not possible to hold that title if you have groups of students you will not teach."

He did not know what to say. I said, "You will teach one class of ninth-graders next year." And he did.

The superintendent told me years later that his son had had George as a teacher and was okay with him. When the superintendent asked his son why he was okay with this teacher, the son said, "Dad, he is an a--hole to everyone. He makes no distinctions. In his classroom, you always know what you are going to get. It is the same every day."

Emotional noise

Emotional realities of the teacher

LOW NOISE		HIGH NOISE
<ul><li>Bonding and attachment style of teacher is secure</li><li>Teacher knows own triggers</li><li>Emotional issues are named accurately</li><li>Discipline and relationships are focused on motivating good behaviors</li></ul>		<ul><li>Bonding and attachment style is insecure</li><li>Teacher often responds to own emotional triggers</li><li>Discipline motivates more bad behaviors</li><li>Relationships with students are minimal or inappropriate</li></ul>

Emotional realities of the classroom

LOW NOISE		HIGH NOISE
<ul><li>Classroom management systems are in place</li><li>Discipline is minimal yet effective</li><li>Strategies are in place to motivate good behaviors</li><li>Processes are in place to deal with holidays</li></ul>		<ul><li>Classroom chaotic and often out of control</li><li>Classroom has favorite students</li><li>Strategies are about survival</li><li>No coherent systems in place</li></ul>

Emotional realities of the 10–15% with the most emotional issues

LOW NOISE		HIGH NOISE
<ul><li>Students are triaged</li><li>A daily contact is made with each student</li><li>Emotional issues are monitored on a weekly basis</li></ul>	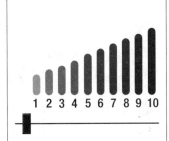	<ul><li>No triage in place</li><li>These students are ostracized, punished, and bullied</li><li>Teacher reacts to incident when it occurs—no preplanning for response</li><li>Rigidity of approach to students, zero tolerance</li></ul>

Sally

Sally was a ninth- and tenth-grade teacher who was also the wife of a local minister. In her early 50s, she was always socially polite, appropriately outgoing, and careful to follow all the directives of the building. She was warm with students and had an orderly control of her classroom. Her pedagogy was sound. Her levels of achievement were not exceptional.

I was the high school English department chair. One day a sophomore girl came to my classroom and said, "Miss, you have to come. There is a problem. The teacher is weaving around the classroom and her speech is munchy and fuzzy. There is something wrong with her."

First of all, if a high school student comes and gets you, there is a *serious* problem. I went over to the classroom, and indeed, Sally was stumbling and her speech was slurred. I said to Sally, "I don't think you are feeling well. Let's go to the nurse's office." I took her there and also found the principal and told him what had happened.

The principal called Sally's husband, and the husband came up to school and picked Sally up. The next day Sally and her husband were in the principal's office, and the husband said to the principal, "If she was taking something, she isn't now. She is fine."

Sally always brought her own thermos of coffee to the classroom. As the story unfolded throughout the rest of the year, she suffered from anxiety and was both taking barbiturates and lacing her coffee with alcohol. She had forgotten how much she had taken, and her involuntary system had slowed down. Sally resigned from her position.

Emotional noise

Emotional realities of the teacher

LOW NOISE		HIGH NOISE
• Bonding and attachment style of teacher is secure		• Bonding and attachment style is insecure
• Teacher knows own triggers		• Teacher often responds to own emotional triggers
• Emotional issues are named accurately		• Discipline motivates more bad behaviors
• Discipline and relationships are focused on motivating good behaviors		• Relationships with students are minimal or inappropriate

Emotional realities of the classroom

LOW NOISE		HIGH NOISE
• Classroom management systems are in place		• Classroom chaotic and often out of control
• Discipline is minimal yet effective		• Classroom has favorite students
• Strategies are in place to motivate good behaviors		• Strategies are about survival
• Processes are in place to deal with holidays		• No coherent systems in place

Emotional realities of the 10–15% with the most emotional issues

LOW NOISE		HIGH NOISE
• Students are triaged		• No triage in place
• A daily contact is made with each student		• These students are ostracized, punished, and bullied
• Emotional issues are monitored on a weekly basis		• Teacher reacts to incident when it occurs—no preplanning for response
		• Rigidity of approach to students, zero tolerance

Delores

Delores was the high school choral director. She had more than 150 students in her program, including several football players, in a small high school. She was known for her extraordinary successes. In the University Interscholastic League contests, her students usually won. When she gave a concert performance, it was as good as any professional performance.

She demanded much from her students, and she got results. The football coach was also a winning football coach, and there was a conflict about time allocation for the students they shared. Periodically both Delores and the coach wanted the students during the same time frames.

To deal with this issue, Delores required her students to sign a commitment form before school started that stated they would commit their time to the choir. She also negotiated with the football coach, and she made sure that the superintendent was behind her.

Her students loved her. She was funny, demanding, and had an incredible expertise in music. If parents questioned her on the commitment she required of her students, she would have a conversation with them, remind them that excellence is a habit, and would ask for the commitment of the parents as well.

Emotional noise

Emotional realities of the teacher

LOW NOISE		HIGH NOISE
▪ Bonding and attachment style of teacher is secure ▪ Teacher knows own triggers ▪ Emotional issues are named accurately ▪ Discipline and relationships are focused on motivating good behaviors		▪ Bonding and attachment style is insecure ▪ Teacher often responds to own emotional triggers ▪ Discipline motivates more bad behaviors ▪ Relationships with students are minimal or inappropriate

Emotional realities of the classroom

LOW NOISE		HIGH NOISE
▪ Classroom management systems are in place ▪ Discipline is minimal yet effective ▪ Strategies are in place to motivate good behaviors ▪ Processes are in place to deal with holidays		▪ Classroom chaotic and often out of control ▪ Classroom has favorite students ▪ Strategies are about survival ▪ No coherent systems in place

Emotional realities of the 10–15% with the most emotional issues

LOW NOISE		HIGH NOISE
▪ Students are triaged ▪ A daily contact is made with each student ▪ Emotional issues are monitored on a weekly basis		▪ No triage in place ▪ These students are ostracized, punished, and bullied ▪ Teacher reacts to incident when it occurs—no preplanning for response ▪ Rigidity of approach to students, zero tolerance

Four issues from adults that impact the emotional dance in the classroom are:

a. The adult's personal bonding and attachment style

b. The adult's energy level

c. The adult's emotional triggers

d. The adult's age and stage of development

Bonding and attachment style of educator

Here are patterns that *might* be seen in a classroom given the teacher's bonding and attachment style:

When the educator is secure and attached ...

- The classroom has boundaries about behaviors. The educator tells a student no.
- The classroom is structured for optimal learning.
- Processes are used and taught.
- The atmosphere is businesslike, compassionate, and focused.
- Discipline is about choices and consequences and not about shame or guilt.
- Individual student needs are acknowledged.
- Relationships of mutual respect promote both relationships and learning.

When the educator is insecure and anxious-ambivalent ...

- Students are often not held accountable for behavior. The educator is hesitant to tell the student no.
- The educator will not have very good boundaries with parents.
- It is very important to the teacher that students like the teacher.
- Learning is secondary to relationships.
- Evaluation makes the teacher anxious. The teacher is very concerned that the administrator likes the teacher.
- The educator may be overwhelmed by demands.

When the educator is insecure and anxious-avoidant ...

- There are more discipline referrals.
- "If you don't learn here, it's not my fault."
- The educator does not like parent-teacher conferences and avoids them.
- More parental complaints occur.
- The educator is less likely to build relationships with students.

When the educator is safe and dangerous ...

- What happens in their classroom/building is not their fault.
- May engage in shame, guilt, dismissal, disdain to/for students/teachers.
- They tend to bully students/teachers.
- Discipline patterns are unpredictable.
- At the secondary level, may be inappropriate with students/staff sexually, morally, legally.
- May openly and disparagingly discuss students/teachers in front of other students/teachers.

Emotional triggers of the educator
Students have emotional triggers. So do adults.

Have you ever asked yourself, "Why did I do that? What was that about?"

What happened is that an inner hurt you did not even know you had got triggered.

The style of bonding and attachment that the educator had as a child and adolescent affects the educator's current relationships, as well as the manner in which the educator builds relationships with students and colleagues. In addition, it affects how discipline is used in the classroom.

The bonding and attachment style you had growing up does not matter. The research is that you can change the impact of it and patterns you use if:

1. You can make a narrative of your life that clearly identifies the positives and negatives of the adults and situations in your life.

2. You can find another adult who will bond with you and validate you.

What does that mean? In the research, if you are not able to look at the adults in your childhood from the point of view of an adult (rather than seeing them as you did when you were the child in the parent-child relationship)—identifying both their assets and liabilities—and identify the core hurts and core values you received from them, then it is not possible for you to leave emotional poverty because you will be blindsided by the core hurts. *It is analogous to having a festering sore that never heals, and if it gets bumped, it bleeds all over again.*

The anxiety-ridden individual has lots of blame for the adults. I am reminded of the cartoon in which a woman is forcing her husband and children to help roll a huge ball of manure up a steep hill. It keeps rolling back to the bottom of the hill. Her husband says to her, "Can't we just leave it here at the bottom of the hill?"

His wife says, "No. My mother gave it to me, and I can't leave it alone."

The avoidant individual is very dismissive of the experience:

- "If I made it through it, so can you."
- "Yeah, we got beaten nearly every day by my mother, but it was good for us."
- "Yeah, my old man beat up on me, but I am okay."

If you don't want to react without knowing why, then here is a challenge:

1. On this timeline, identify five key memories/events/happenings in your life. For example: a death, marriage, birth of a child, college, groom did not show to my wedding, major car accident, Ms. Benton my fourth-grade teacher, homecoming queen, etc. Put an X on the timeline for each one. Label it if you wish. (Research indicates that individual personality is fairly shaped by 29 years of age.)

Early: Birth–9   Adolescence: 10–18   Early adulthood: 19–30

2. On this timeline, identify the five key people in your life who shaped your core self. Use initials to identify them.

Early: Birth–9   Adolescence: 10–18   Early adulthood: 19–30

3. For each X in Question 1, identify the core inner hurts and core inner values you got from each X.

4. For each set of initials in Question 2, identify the core inner hurts and core inner values you received from each person.

INNER HURTS	INNER VALUES
Less than	Importance
Separate from	Value
Disregarded	Worthiness
Unlovable	Equality
Accused	Flexibility
Rejected	Resilience
Powerless	Ability to recognize core values in others
Inadequate	
Unimportant	

What triggers a reaction in us is a core hurt we did not know we had.

Identifying these hurts helps avoid a reaction we do not want to have.

The same inner hurts tend to show up repeatedly. Those are your triggers. When you are faced with anything that makes the amygdala think that your current experience is similar to a past experience, those same inner hurts will surface again and you will react. Remember, what fires together in the brain wires together. You will have an automatic response because that neural pathway is already established.

To get beyond the trigger, you must identify how those inner hurts can be addressed to become core strengths through a process called validation, which we'll discuss later in the book.

> The emotional classroom dance is also affected by the energy level of the educator.
>
> Teaching requires incredible levels of energy.

Energy and stress

When we look at our energy in terms of stress, we can see how our bodies constantly react to our internal and external environments. We require certain amounts of energy to eat, sleep, and survive. Our thoughts and our behaviors claim energy. Working, studying, dealing with our children, and spending time with friends all call for the use of energy.

Everyday situations produce stress. Our beliefs, our expectations, and our relationships demand a great deal of energy. Trying to do the right thing in accordance with our values (cultural, social, religious), fulfilling our own and others' expectations, and establishing and keeping up with relationships can leave us tired and frustrated. Although we're usually capable of juggling all our daily tasks, they can sometimes create conflicts and dilemmas to which we reluctantly devote our contingent energy and time. Sometimes our efforts do not have the desired outcome—but we feel we must devote the energy anyway. We resent that; it makes us angry. Our truest and deepest needs are not getting met, and so we devote more energy to our anger and resentments, to our fears and worries. When that happens, usually the first thing depleted is our contingent energy.

We can choose how we use our energy

Now that we know how energy is generated and how it can make us feel good or bad, we can work on choosing how we want to use this energy—and decide on the attitudes and behaviors we will adopt to deal with our responsibilities and daily stressors.

Key points

1. When there is general compatibility between our energy and our time allocations, we tend to be happier.

2. As long as we freely choose to allocate our energy to the parts of our lives that bring us satisfaction and meaning—and most of our expectations are met—we tend to be happier.

3. As long as we choose to address our anxieties and fears in a healthy manner, we tend to be happier.

4. As long as we are consciously aware of how to best handle stress, we can use our energy wisely and find better solutions to our problems.

5. We tend to be happiest when there is contingent energy for the people, activities, and things that bring us joy, zest, and meaning.

Energy (over the life span)

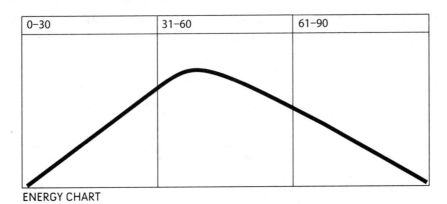

0–30	31–60	61–90

ENERGY CHART

Available energy usually rises until individuals are in their early 30s. Until we're in our 30s, many of us believe we have unlimited energy and privilege. Most such expectations seem to be of things we think will come to us freely, or at the very least, we expect that there will be enough energy to acquire and access what we desire. Privileges and expectations are often related to our experience of growing up. *Furthermore, we make commitments to the future (for example, children and debt), assuming we will have the energy to address those commitments. Sometimes, however, as situations take on multipliers we didn't anticipate, the responsibilities can become overwhelming.*

Until most people are in their early 30s, there is less responsibility than there is energy. However, when they get into their 30s, especially when they have children and/or a demanding career, responsibilities usually begin to increase and intensify.

Responsibilities (over the life span)

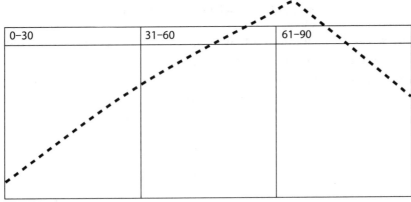

0–30	31–60	61–90

RESPONSIBILITY CHART

In other words, once we hit our 30s and 40s, our natural energy starts to decline, and our responsibilities tend to pick up. Responsibilities include career demands, demands from children and aging parents, health issues, financial constraints, unemployment, loss of loved ones, etc.

And then our chart looks like this:

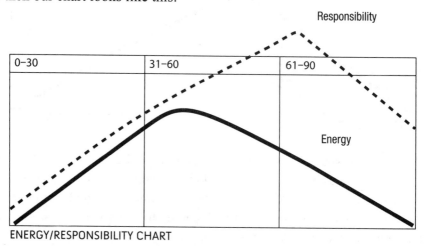

ENERGY/RESPONSIBILITY CHART

As we move into our 30s, our responsibilities usually increase and can outweigh our energy. However, the beliefs of youth tend to still be with us—especially the belief that our energy will continue to grow. So we accept more responsibilities.

As we begin to address the responsibilities, we often shift energy into anxiety, which then depletes our contingent energy. In that natural process, we begin to lose the very parts of ourselves that allowed us to live. We feel overwhelmed. And over time, responsibilities continue to increase as energy decreases. Unlike youth, when there always seemed to be more energy than we knew what to do with, maturity's challenge is to handle more responsibility with fewer resources. It takes great personal strength and balance to be able to do so.

The issue with responsibilities is that we often accept them for a long time into the future without understanding the ramifications of such decisions. Sometimes responsibilities are thrust upon us without our consent or permission, but other times we make commitments because we love someone and/or we feel called to serve. And sometimes responsibilities are simply about survival.

How would you draw your responsibility line? What contributes to your responsibility line? Add yours to the chart below.

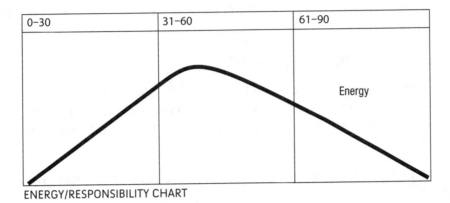

0–30	31–60	61–90

Energy

ENERGY/RESPONSIBILITY CHART

What responsibilities do you have because of earlier commitments? What is the relationship now between your responsibilities and your energy?

If there is a big (and growing) gap between available energy and a high level of responsibility, then living can increasingly become empty and colorless. The days are gray. Hope is nonexistent. The purpose and joy for living are largely gone. Each day becomes a struggle to survive. The following story illustrates how this can happen.

A story: Burned out

Stephanie is an elementary school principal. She is at school every morning by 7 a.m. and leaves at 5:30 p.m. Her husband, a retired educator, is in intensive care again. He has chronic obstructive pulmonary disease (COPD) and prostate cancer. Stephanie goes directly from her job to the hospital to be with him. She buys both of them food—he does not like the hospital food. She stays with him until 10:30 p.m. She goes home to bed and gets up the next morning at 5:30 a.m. to get ready to go to school. On the weekends she spends most of her time at the hospital.

Stephanie is exhausted every day. She simply has no contingent energy. Every day is about survival.

Age and stages of adult development

Yet another factor in the emotional noise in the classroom is where the educator is in terms of their own adult development. Sometimes you have two teachers who are at very different stages of development, as the following story illustrates.

A story: Simply devastated

A friend of mine was working with a high school English department. One of the teachers was a beginning teacher in her 20s. Another teacher in the department was a veteran teacher in her mid-40s. They got into an argument, and the teacher in her 20s started crying.

She said to the older teacher, "You are no friend of mine. You should not think or say that!"

The veteran teacher patted her heart melodramatically and said, "Oh, that tugs at my heartstrings. I am simply devastated!" And then the veteran teacher laughed.

Two very different stages of adult development! In the research, adults in their 20s are very concerned with what you "should" do to be an adult. By the time you are in your mid-40s, you have had a wealth of experience, and you know that not everyone is going to be your friend or agree with you. Experience becomes a huge factor in your decisions.

The emotional noise in that particular English department was quite high. The teachers in that department had difficulty working together for several reasons. One of the reasons was that the teachers were at very different stages and facing very different adult development tasks.

Adults, like children, go through different stages of development as they age. Gail Sheehy, in her book *Passages: Predictable Crises of Adult Life,* has identified some of these issues in her research with adults.

To remember:

1. These stages are not prescriptive but descriptive.

2. These stages represent patterns that individuals at that age *tend to have.* Not everyone will experience that age in that way.

3. "During each of these ... [stages], how we feel about our way of living will undergo subtle changes in four areas of perception. One is the interior sense of self in relation to others. A second is the proportion of safeness to

danger we feel in our lives. A third is our perception of time—do we have plenty of it, or are we beginning to feel that time is running out? Last, there will be some shift at the gut level in our sense of aliveness or stagnation."[97]

4. "Times of crisis, of disruption or constructive change, are not only predictable but desirable. They mean growth."[98]

5. A person may need to experience a crisis before identity can be fully developed.

6. According to behavioral theorists, both boys and girls have their primary attachment to the mother.

7. "When the tasks of one period remain largely unmet, they will complicate or interfere with the work on the tasks of the next period. In the extreme case, development may be impaired to such a degree that the person cannot truly enter the new period."[99]

Basic adult development tasks

Regardless of race, country of origin, birth order, etc., these are developmental tasks that every adult faces.

Identity – Who am I?

Intimacy – Who am I in relationship to another?

Independence/autonomy – What can I do on my own?

Purpose/meaning – Why am I alive?

Work/role – What value do I bring?

Limitations of time – What do I do with the time I have?

Aging/death – How do I deal with the aging and death of others? How do I deal with my own aging and end-of-life issues?

All of these adult development tasks create emotional responses. Every individual has a choice to ignore or delay the development, but the issue will keep returning to be addressed.

Age frame	Tasks/issues/key questions
18–22 'Pulling up roots'	**Key question: What am I going to do with my life?** Four tasks: Find a peer-group role, a sex role, an occupation, and a worldview/set of beliefs. Establish autonomy and identity. De-idealize the parent or parent substitute in order to start trusting own judgment. Big focus on what you do not want to do or be. In 2017, 30% of individuals under the age of 30 lived at home with their parents. These developmental tasks occur even if the individual is living at home. They may be delayed, but the issues of identity, intimacy, occupation, and a worldview/set of beliefs tend to develop.
22–28 'Trying 20s'	**Key question: What should I do to be an adult?** Tasks: Shape a dream, prepare for life's work, find a mentor, develop intimacy with another. Have a deep fear that choices are irrevocable. Strong belief that I will never be like my parents, that partners will grow together at equal speeds. A time of competing forces—stability and structure versus exploration and experimentation. Reasons for marriage in the 20s include: the need for safety, the need to fill some vacancy in yourself, the need to get away from home, the need for prestige or practicality.[100] The presence or absence of a mentor at this time "has enormous impact on development ... The lack of mentors ... is a great developmental handicap."[101] There is a tendency to marry someone who has many characteristics of or plays a similar role to one of our parents.
28–32 'Passage to the 30s'	**Key question: Do I agree with the adult that I am becoming?** Tasks: Revisit the decisions involving identity, intimacy, independence, marriage (lots of first divorces occur at this time), children (to have or not to have), career choices (do I really want to do this?), etc. Strong belief that there is still time to do it all. Women see it as a last chance in terms of children, career, and life path. Men often press the accelerator harder. Marriage satisfaction decreases. "For the past 50 years, Americans have been most likely to break out of wedlock when the man is about 30 and the woman is about 28."[102] Learns that intelligence is not as well rewarded as loyalty. Learns that not all difficulties can be solved with willpower and intellect.

(continued on next page)

(continued from previous page)

Age frame	Tasks/issues/key questions
32–39 **'Settling down'**	**Key question: How do I achieve balance?** Tasks: "To sort out the qualities we want to retain from our childhood models, to blend them with the qualities and capacities that distinguish us as individuals, and to fit all this back together in some broader form."[103] Women come "to understand that it is probably not possible for a woman to work out a combination of the two careers (domestic and extra-familial) until 30 or 35."[104] Conflict between safety and autonomy, freedom and stability. Time is a huge issue—there is not enough. Squeezed between demands of children, career, aging parents, family dynamics. Strong defense of current beliefs. Fairly certain that their understanding/worldview is correct.
35–45 **'Authenticity crisis'** **'Danger and opportunity'** **'The adolescence of adulthood'**	**Key questions: Why am I doing this? What do I really believe?** Tasks: Aliveness versus stagnation. Shift in the sense of time—health, career, mortality (will not live forever). Changes happening in self and in others. New wrinkles appear every day. Taking apart the dream and its illusions to spark renewal. Hormonal changes: Males start producing less testosterone, which allows estrogen to play more of a role (become more nurturing). Females produce less estrogen, and testosterone plays more of a role (become more assertive). "The loss of youth, the faltering of physical powers we have always taken for granted, the fading purpose of stereotyped roles by which we have thus far identified ourselves, the spiritual dilemma of having no absolute answers—any or all of these shocks can throw us into crisis."[105] "Every loose end not resolved in previous passages will resurface to haunt us. These demons may lead us into private hells of depression, sexual promiscuity, power chasing, hypochondria, self-destructive acts (alcoholism, drug taking, car accidents, suicide), and violent swings of mood. All are well documented as rising during the middle years."[106] Must do some grieving for the old self. We do a gut-level reintegration of self, and we face up to our own inevitable death. **"37–42 are the peak years of anxiety for almost everyone."[107]**

(continued on next page)

(continued from previous page)

Age frame	Tasks/issues/key questions
42–55 **'Renewal or resignation'**	**Key question: What must I do?**
	Tasks: Experience becomes a major tool with which decisions are made. Freedom to be independent, one's own self, within a relationship. No one can totally understand who I am. Parents are forgiven. Children are "released" to be adults. Dealing with aging.
	Key understanding that there is not enough time anymore, so what are my priorities for the time I have left?
	Motto of this stage is "no more bulls--t."[108]
	For men, "the 40s are a time for discovering the emotive parts of themselves that didn't fit with the posture of the strong, dynamic, rational young men they were supposed to be at 25."[109]
	Remember that "middle-aged men and women are the 'norm-bearers and decision-makers,' and that while 'they live in a society … oriented toward youth,' it is 'controlled by the middle-aged' … After 45, most people who have allowed themselves the authenticity crisis are ready to accept entry to middle age and to enjoy its many prerogatives."[110]
	"The crux of it is to see, to feel, and finally to know that none of us can aspire to fulfillment through someone else."[111]
55–70 **'Integrity … despair and disgust'**	**Key questions: What is my legacy? What am I going to do next? How can I give back?**
	Tasks: Address career questions. Do I retire or do I stay? If I am forced out of my career, what do I do? If I retire, what will I do next? Health issues. Financial issues: Can I afford to retire? What did/does my life mean? Family commitments and issues—raising grandchildren, etc.
	More time is devoted to health issues—maintenance, repair, serious illness, etc.
	According to insurance actuaries, more than one third of individuals who retire are deceased within 18 months.[112]
	Important to develop new friends—particularly those younger than you. Friends you have had for a long time die.
	Erikson identified this time as one of gathering greater authenticity for the life lived versus seeing one's life as a mistake, a waste of time, without meaning or purpose.
	Integrity makes the 70s one of the happiest times for many adults, while others may become trapped in despair and disgust.

"Everyone has difficulty with the steps of inner growth, even when the outer obstacles appear easily surmountable. What's more, the prizes of our society are reserved for outer, not inner, achievements. Scant are the trophies given for reconciling all the forces that compete to direct our development, although working toward such a reconciliation hour by demanding hour, day by triumphant day, year by exacting year is what underlies all growth of the personality. A great deal of behavioral red tape can be cut through once people have developed judgment enriched by both inner and outer experience. It is this striking improvement in the exercise of judgment."[113]

How does adult development impact the classroom and campus?

20s	30s
■ Very concerned with what they "should" do.	■ Very interested in the latest research. Use it in decision making.
■ Unfamiliar with discipline patterns, response choices, and establishing boundaries. Coaching helps.	■ Need to argue and discuss a new idea before implementation.
■ Very uncertain about how to deal with parents. Helps to have faculty meetings to role-play parent meetings.	■ Squeezed by time demands, children, and career advancement.
■ Benefit significantly from a good mentor.	■ Need conversations about career advancement.
■ Need to be protected from veteran educators who are rigid and negative.	■ Will pursue advanced degrees.
■ Need good sources of practical advice.	■ After 10 years of teaching, tend to have expertise, and many responses are at the level of automaticity.
Emotional noise may increase because of uncertainty of patterns and responses.	*Emotional noise may increase because of multiple demands on energy and squeezed time.*

(continued on next page)

(continued from previous page)

40s	50s
▪ Care about research but will only use it if it makes sense with their experience. ▪ Rely upon experience and patterns of response that have worked over time. ▪ Extreme fatigue and little patience for "BS." ▪ Excellent at being "scouts" for new approaches before they are accepted and implemented. ▪ Recognize classroom patterns almost before they start. Experts at preventive approaches. *Emotional noise may be increased by too many changes: "This too will pass." Or a personal crisis may occur that diverts focus and energy.*	▪ Make excellent mentors. ▪ Squeezed by time—aging parents, children returning home, grandchildren issues. ▪ Health issues may surface. ▪ Slow to implement change if close to retirement. ▪ Preoccupation with what comes next. ▪ Excellent sounding boards for student analysis and response. ▪ For excellent teachers, prowess and expertise becomes phenomenal. *Emotional noise may increase because of squeezed time, less energy, health issues, fatigue with office politics, friends and family who die, etc.*

If an adult is going through a crisis, a great deal of energy is expended to deal with the crisis. It simply means that the focus and energy necessary to address the emotional realities of the classroom may be thin. Given the composition of the building, if 10–15% of students have intense emotional issues, the combination may trigger emotional responses in the adult that are less than optimal. It is very beneficial for educators to understand that they themselves go through emotional stages of development just as their students do.

What does this mean in the classroom? What do you have to do to address the emotional dance?

1. Remember that there are a lot more people in the room than you knew.

2. Triage your students. Ninety percent of discipline referrals come from 10–15% of the students. *Know those students well.* Identify who in your class leans toward "safe and dangerous." Watch them carefully.

3. Know your own triggers so that your brain can stay integrated and regulated.

4. Manage the emotional noise level in your classroom. Know that before and after holidays, it will be higher.

5. Be aware of your own bonding and attachment tendencies.

6. Identify which problems can be solved and which ones need to be managed.

7. Be aware of where you are in your own stage of life. What emotional issues are you dealing with outside of the school that come with you into the classroom?

What do you do about the emotional noise in the classroom and on the campus?

Many of these are context issues that create underlying noise.

In the classroom

Issue	Suggested interventions
Classroom management procedures	Use the classroom management chart in *Research-Based Strategies* or see Appendix B.
Classroom composition, students with persistent emotional issues	Has triage of the difficult students been done? Is the percentage of difficult students higher than 15%? If so, some changes need to be made, if possible.
Who the students brought into the room in their head	For the students who make the most emotional noise, who is in their head?
Who the teacher brought into the room with them/energy level of the adult	Self-reflection.
Stages of adult development	Know the tasks of adult development for that age range.
Bonding and attachment styles of students	Identify the interventions that tend to work better with those students.
Bonding and attachment style of teacher	What are the coaching and support systems for adults?
Pre- and post-holiday noise	What procedures are in place when they walk into your room? Is there board work that they begin immediately? Do you avoid assignments that create shame, e.g., "Write about your summer vacation," or "How many gifts did you get at the holidays?"

At the campus level

Issue	Suggested interventions
Campus triage plan	10–15% of students triaged. Referral system available outside of campus.
Provide role models for all students.	At secondary level, have both male and female administrators.
Pre- and post-holiday noise	What procedures are in place when students return? Are they greeted at the door?
Recess/lunchroom protocols	No student eats or plays alone.
Routines for beginning and end of school	Are those in place and enforced?
Bus/pickup/driving routines	Are those in place and enforced?
Assembly protocols	Are those in place and enforced?
At secondary level, whether you are an affluent or high-poverty school, who sways the student population?	In high-poverty schools, student culture is heavily influenced by males. There tend to be more physical fights. In affluent high schools, female students tend to influence the school culture more heavily. There is more social bullying and social exclusion. It is one of the reasons that the majority of mass school shootings occur in affluent high schools.
Bathroom cleanliness/mirrors/access	The cleanliness of bathrooms indicates the amount of respect that adults give to students. Also, many fights involve students at the mirrors (particularly females). Do the toilets work? Are there doors on the stalls?
Routines for safety/fire drills/lockdowns, etc.	Are those in place and rehearsed?
Number of exclusionary processes by race, gender, class, and country of origin—based on identity	Need to make sure that every student has a group to belong to. Ensure that processes are not discriminatory or exclusionary according to who the student "is"—identity. Need to have behavioral controls (what the student does).

7 More Factors in Emotional Development

How might additional factors in the external environment contribute to emotional poverty?

Not all emotional development comes from the bonding and attachment to the caregiver. What are some of the additional factors that impact emotional development?

In this chapter we will be covering:

- Parenting issues: parental alienation in divorce, structure and function of family, little or no discipline, fatherless households, emotional neglect, emotional distress in affluent households
- Biochemical issues, mental illness, personality disorders (narcissistic or borderline)
- Addictions, including screen addiction, and their impact on mental health and brain development
- Survival/financial poverty environments
- Neighborhood effects and early puberty
- ACE: adverse childhood experiences and abuse
- Death/war/violence

Parenting issues
Family structure and function

It is very important to distinguish between family structure and family function. Family *structure* is the configuration of the family, e.g., single parent, two parent, blended family (his, hers, and ours), single-parent household headed by the father, single-parent household headed by the mother, etc. Family function is the extent to which the following five needs are met for children under the age of 18: material necessities, learning, self-respect, peer relationships, and harmony and stability.[114]

It is very possible for a child to have a two-parent household that is unable to have family function. And it is very possible for a child to have a single-parent household and have high family function.

Family function is heavily impacted by two things: low income and high violence. When the family function is not occurring, then the emotional damage is greater.

No boundaries, lots of choices, no consequences

Of incredible damage to children is failure to establish the internal self-regulation that is necessary for adulthood.

Jordan Peterson, a Canadian clinical psychologist, states,

> Children can be damaged as much or more by a lack of incisive attention as they are by abuse, mental or physical. This is damage by omission, rather than commission, but it is no less severe and long-lasting. Children are damaged when their "mercifully" inattentive parents fail to make them sharp and observant and awake and leave them, instead, in an unconscious and undifferentiated state. Children are damaged when those charged with their care, afraid of any conflict or upset, no longer dare to correct them, and leave them without guidance ... Such children are chronically ignored by their peers.[115]

Financially affluent households

Stosny states that emotional abuse is much more impactful than physical violence.

One of the realities in high-income households is the drive for competition. Social exclusion is the weapon of choice in many affluent households. And it is brutal. You are "less than" and "separate from." When you have the money but not the connections, then the only way you can have the opportunities you want for your child is for your child to be "better" than anyone else. The competitive drive is very respected and tied to entrance into the "right" colleges and universities.

Furthermore, in affluent households, the understanding is that if you have an emotional issue, it is to be shared *only* with a professional who is discreet. Emotional expression is muted and careful.

Emotional neglect can be present if the child has very little exposure to the adults and is raised by the nanny. If the relationship with the nanny is a long-time relationship and the child is bonded to the nanny, then the child is more emotionally secure.

There is increased use of Adderall in more affluent households. Adderall helps with concentration and weight loss. I mentioned previously that I worked with one high school in a North Shore suburb of Chicago that was quite affluent and had about 1,500 students. That particular high school had, on the average, five students a week who had to be hospitalized in psychiatric institutions.

There is an interplay that goes on in very affluent neighborhoods that involves competition and children. Old money (families that have been wealthy for two generations or more) and new money (families where the parents are the first generation to achieve wealth) often live in the same neighborhoods, but they do not think the same way. New money is about income, and old money is about connections. Adults who come from wealth usually put their children in private school or even private boarding school. People with new money often have their children in public school for part of their school years but may switch them to private school later.

What drives the competition involving children is college admittance, sports, and talent opportunities. The opportunities for parents to increase their exposure to greater career and social opportunities through their children's performance is another driving force.

Seventy percent of wealthy families have lost their wealth by the second generation.[116] Old money tends to live off of assets. Some from old money do not work for income. Over time, given inflation and the distribution of the money to subsequent generations, old money has less cash and income. However, old money comes with connections and memberships to private clubs, colleges, universities, decorators, investment gurus, etc.

Of course, private clubs, universities, etc. need cash and revenue to operate. This means new money and old money often mix at social events that raise money for a charitable cause. New money is often carefully screened and invited into private clubs simply for the infusion of cash.

For example, imagine you are new money and you are invited to join the country club. Your daughter takes private tennis lessons and becomes very good. She starts playing club tennis and winning tournaments, and then she wins a couple of state titles. This makes your country club look very good, but more importantly, people at the club who have more money and connections than you start going out of their way to meet you. That results in invitations to participate in other social events where you meet people who can advance your career with promotions, offers from other firms, board appointments, etc.

The pressure on children to perform can be very intense, which creates a huge level of anxiety.

Sometimes the pressure doesn't come from parents or from other students. I was once the principal of a very affluent elementary school. It was a public school, but the price of housing in the district was so high that it was really more like a private school. One day a parent came to me and said, "My son will not be here for the next three Wednesdays. He is taking private baseball pitching lessons with … " and named a famous Major League Baseball pitcher. Taking lessons from someone that famous could make anyone anxious!

Sometimes the pressure is the result of thinking the requirements are stricter than they really are. I had a third-grade boy in my office sobbing uncontrollably on the day of the state test. When I finally got him calmed down, he told me that he had to have a perfect score on the test. I explained to him how the test would be scored, and I told him that he could miss a couple and still be at the very top.

At that affluent elementary school, I would constantly have parents in my office. The reason many of them came was to make sure that their children were at the very top, as close to perfect as possible. As I noted earlier, Suniya Luthar at Arizona State University "has found that privileged youths are among the most emotionally distressed young people in America. 'These kids are incredibly anxious and perfectionistic,' she says, but there's 'contempt and scorn for the idea that kids who have it all might be hurting.'"[117]

Emotional neglect and 'parentification' of a child

Emotional abuse occurs when the child is not attuned to a primary adult or is the object of psychological control. If the child is criticized, humiliated, compared unfavorably to siblings, or takes the parent role in the household because the parent is not available (two jobs, incarceration, physical or mental illness, or absence may be the reason), then the emotional development that the child needs to have is subverted/delayed by the needs of the adult.

Characteristics of children who have been "parentified" include the following: feeling responsible for the parent's feelings and well-being, having indifferent parents, being asked to take on adult roles, being the target of an unhappy parent, and being blamed, criticized, demeaned, or devalued.

Parental alienation in divorce

Increasingly courts are dealing with parental alienation issues during divorce using supervised visits by a court-appointed psychologist. In a non-divorce situation, the parents bond to take care of the child. In a divorce, the two parents are no longer bonded, but in a healthy divorced situation, each parent has a bond with the child. In parental alienation, one parent will insist that they are the only one who should bond with the child and that the other parent should be excluded.

Research by Childress indicates that in parental alienation, the parent doing the alienating is usually the problem parent. The problem parent will often paint the other parent as the problem through a set of very subtle insinuations and generalities.[118] This often becomes a court problem. Schools often become involved because one parent will not want a child to go with another parent even though that parent has visitation rights to see the child.

Fatherless sons

Males who grow up without a father—because of death, divorce, incarceration, abandonment, etc.—do not see the responses that a male makes to everyday life. This impacts the emotional development of the male.

In the research, sons in fatherless households are:

- More likely to be aggressive
- More likely to be depressed
- More prone to low self-esteem
- More likely to do poorly in school
- More likely to use drugs
- More likely to be incarcerated and commit suicide[119]

It should be noted that the presence of positive adult males, even when there is not a father, can make a huge difference. My own father's father died when my father was one year old. His mother had several brothers, and they stepped in to become "fathers" to my father. This meant he had male role models present on a daily basis in his life, even though his father was dead. My father was successful and a good father himself. He received a lot of emotional development from his uncles.

Adverse childhood experiences

Some of the best research on this subject has been the ACE (adverse childhood experiences) research. It is a simple 10-question quiz, and each item that you check as true gets one point.

Adverse childhood experience (ACE) questionnaire
Finding your ACE score

- Ten categories of adverse childhood experiences—physical and sexual abuse, physical and emotional neglect, household dysfunction (incarceration, mental illness, addiction), etc.
- ACE score—one point for each category of trauma
- A score of 4 or higher—twice as likely to smoke, seven times as likely to have sex before age 15 and to be alcoholics

Question 1. Did a parent or other adult in the household often ...

Swear at you, insult you, put you down, or humiliate you?

or

Act in a way that made you afraid that you might be physically hurt?

Yes or No If yes, enter 1 _____

Question 2. Did a parent or other adult in the household often ...

Push, grab, slap, or throw something at you?

or

Ever hit you so hard that you had marks or were injured?

Yes or No If yes, enter 1 _____

Question 3. Did an adult or person at least five years older than you ever ...

Touch or fondle you or have you touch their body in a sexual way?

or

Try to or actually have oral, anal, or vaginal sex with you?

Yes or No If yes, enter 1 _____

Question 4. Did you often feel that ...

No one in your family loved you or thought you were important or special?

or

Your family didn't look out for each other, feel close to each other, or support each other?

Yes or No If yes, enter 1 _____

Question 5. Did you often feel that ...

You didn't have enough to eat, had to wear dirty clothes, and had no one to protect you?

or

Your parents were too drunk or high to take care of you or take you to the doctor if you needed it?

Yes or No If yes, enter 1 _____

Question 6. Were your parents ever separated or divorced?

Yes or No If yes, enter 1 _____

Question 7. Was your mother or stepmother:

Often pushed, grabbed, slapped, or had something thrown at her?

or

Sometimes or often kicked, bitten, hit with a fist, or hit with something hard?

or

Ever repeatedly hit over at least a few minutes or threatened with a gun or knife?

Yes or No If yes, enter 1 _____

Question 8. Did you live with anyone who was a problem drinker or alcoholic or who used street drugs?

Yes or No If yes, enter 1 _____

Question 9. Was a household member depressed or mentally ill or did a household member attempt suicide?

Yes or No If yes, enter 1 _____

Question 10. Did a household member go to prison?

Yes or No If yes, enter 1 _____

Now add up your "Yes" answers:

_____ **This is your ACE score.**

ACE study and problems at school

- **ACE score of 0:** Only 3% had learning or behavioral problems.
- **ACE score of 4 or higher:** 51% had learning or behavioral problems.[120]

ACE study and juveniles in detention (1,000 in the study)

- The majority had an ACE score of 6 or higher.
- Sixty-six percent had a diagnosable psychiatric disorder.
- The average score on a standardized vocabulary test was fifth percentile.[121]

Mental illness, biochemical issues, and borderline/narcissistic personality disorders

Freud defined mental health as having the ability to love and to work. In the field of mental health, there is general acceptance of a continuum. About 90% of individuals are considered "sane"—i.e., they can work and love. About 5–6% of individuals have a personality disorder—i.e., they have difficulty working and loving. About 3–4% of individuals are considered "insane"—i.e., they cannot work and love in a predictable manner.

90% of the population	5–6% of the population	3–4% of the population
Sane: Can love and work	Personality disorder: Has difficulty working and loving	Insane: Cannot work or love

Both borderline and narcissist personality disorders are known to result in emotionally unstable personalities. A person with narcissistic personality disorder fears rejection. A person with borderline personality disorder fears abandonment. The research indicates that these disorders develop during the bonding and attachment process before the age of 3, although there is research to indicate that there may be biochemical issues as well. Characteristics include: impulsive or dangerous behaviors, distorted self-image, idealization and devaluations, and being overwhelmed by rage, anger, and alienation.

People with borderline and/or narcissistic personality disorder often have these identifiers: very intelligent, very charming, but can change in a second to rage, anger, and alienation. Often there is an addiction involved. Kernberg indicated that individuals with borderline and/or narcissistic personality disorder "are especially deficient in genuine feelings of sadness and mournful longing ... [the deficiency] emerges as anger and resentment loaded with revengeful wishes rather than real sadness."[122]

Parents and students with personality disorders are very difficult to address. They have two characteristics in particular: No solution ever works for very long, and they take up lots and lots and lots of time from lots and lots and lots of people. They are often in the category of safe and dangerous.

Intermixed in all of this range of sanity to insanity are varying degrees of biochemical issues—depression, anxiety, etc. Sometimes no matter what the intervention is, it simply doesn't work. You may be dealing with a biochemical issue.

What are some indicators it may be a biochemical issue?

- The behavior occurs without warning and often without provocation.
- The behavior isn't predictable; there's no pattern.
- The behavior has no advantage for the student. In other words, there isn't a payoff for the behavior. The student doesn't gain anything by engaging in the behavior.
- The behavior often alienates other students.
- The behavior doesn't respond to any cognitive interventions (as would behaviors that are controlled by one's thinking).

Biochemical issues are often physical illnesses that affect thinking, emotions, and behavior. An analogous condition would be diabetes. A person has diabetes because the pancreas does not produce enough insulin, or it may not produce insulin at all. By obtaining insulin from an external source, the person can live a productive life. It is the same with biochemical issues. When individuals can ingest the needed chemicals from an external source, they can be very productive.

At least five disorders are considered biochemical. These are:

- Schizophrenia
- Obsessive-compulsive disorder (OCD)
- Attention-deficit/hyperactivity disorder (ADHD)
- Major depressive disorder (depression)
- Bipolar disorder

The "bible" followed in the mental health field to diagnose disorders is the *Diagnostic and Statistical Manual of Mental Disorders,* fifth edition (DSM-5).[123] It is published by the American Psychiatric Association. This manual is highly technical. *Clinician's Thesaurus: The Guide to Conducting Interviews and Writing Psychological Reports,* by Edward L. Zuckerman, is much more helpful due to its "translation" to more understandable language. The *Clinician's Thesaurus* contains many useful questions and criteria for discussion.[124]

Please note: An accurate diagnosis can be made only by a trained developmental pediatrician, a psychiatrist, or an individual otherwise certified in the area of mental health.

Addiction

Addiction of any kind—shopping, eating, smoking, drugs (legal or illegal), screen, pornography, sexual, gambling, etc.—can be a behavior that becomes habituated over time, establishing neural pathways that are easily accessed. Some addictions have a biochemical basis as well.

Many educators are not aware of the lasting effects on students that an addicted parent has. The effects follow students into adult life, and they often contribute to many of the patterns listed below.

Screen addiction

One of the biggest addictions that is occurring right now with adolescents and young adults is screen addiction.

Screen addiction changes the brain:

- "[Internet addiction] is associated with structural and functional changes in brain regions involving emotional processing, executive attention, decision making, and cognitive control."[125]

- It results in gray matter atrophy (loss of processing), "spotty" white matter (loss of communication), impaired cognitive functioning (reduced impulse inhibition and insensitivity to loss), and cravings and impaired dopamine function (reward processing and addiction).[126]

"The new world of addictive technology … is indeed the equivalent of ubiquitous 'electronic heroin.'"[127] "According to [advocacy group] Common Sense, teens average nine hours of media a day, and tweens average six … A recent study of eighth-graders by Jean Twenge … found that heavy users are 56% more likely to say they are unhappy, 27% more likely to be depressed, and 35% more likely to have a risk factor for suicide."[128]

Death

The loss of a sibling or parent when you are young is life changing. As I mentioned before, according to Virginia Satir, the dead person plays more of a role in family dynamics after their death than they did when they were alive.[129] A large percentage of divorces occur when a child dies. In the research, the death of a parent is most impactful if the child is between the ages of 12 and 14.

When I was a principal, a man walked into my office at 7 a.m. and said, "Rob is with me." Rob was a sixth-grade student. The man continued, "I am his neighbor. His dad died last night in a car accident, and Rob insisted on coming to school. Now he will not get out of the car, and I have to go on to work. I don't know why he wanted to come to school."

I said to the neighbor, "He came to school because he wants to know that somewhere in his life things are somewhat normal. He knows his life will never be the same again, and he wants to be where something is the same."

I went to the car, opened the door, and said to Rob, "Get out of the car and come with me." He did.

When he got to my office, I said to him, "Anytime today that you need to leave, just come down to my office. Do you want to talk to the counselor?"

He said, "No."

I said, "Okay. Just remember you can leave when you need to do so. But make sure that I know that you need to leave. You have to let me know. You cannot just walk out of the building."

In all of these situations, the key ingredient in an individual's ability to negotiate the environment with minimal emotional scarring seems to be a relationship of mutual respect with an adult. Key questions for students are: Do you have one good adult in your life? Do you have one adult who cares about you? Do you have one adult you care about?

What does this mean in the classroom?

Are you going to know *everything* about every student? No. That is not possible.

But you should know enough about each student to begin to know if there is a shift or change in their emotional reality. I knew a middle school teacher who never knew the names of his students—even by the end of the year. Knowing their names is a place to start.

Recently, my husband and I went to a new church, one that his son's family attends. We had already been seated, and we were saving seats for the rest of the family. At least three different people came up to us, greeted us, and talked to us, working to find out why we were there and how we were doing. After the service, I said to my husband, "This is a part of their security detail. Ever since that church shooting in Texas, they are assigning their own members to help with security. This church is using their own members to find anyone who is not familiar, and they are assessing whether the newcomers are safe or not." The minister walked along the front rows of people in the church and shook hands with everyone, again assessing security and safety.

It is that kind of attention to students that we will need to begin to use to keep everyone safe and to assess the emotional realities of our students.

The point of all of this is that external experiences have an impact on emotional development as well. It is not possible to mitigate every issue for every student, *but the way we handle the emotional upsets can be the difference between developing a strong inner self and the motivation for good behavior versus further developing a weak inner self and the motivation for bad behavior.*

Validation

How do I motivate good behaviors?
How do I identify the behaviors that can
only be managed and not changed?

•

It is very difficult to change a behavior. To change
a behavior, change the motivation for behavior.

Here is what happens in the motivation of good behavior: When people experience something that taps an inner hurt, they are able to realize that this behavior or comment reflects more on the other person than on themselves. The brain is regulated and integrated, and a strong inner self is tapped.

People in this position either do not respond, or they respond calmly and without anger. This allows them to see the situation with compassion and to use validation if possible. In future interactions with the individual who triggered the inner hurt, they are able to identify appropriate boundaries, consequences, or support.

What motivates good behavior?

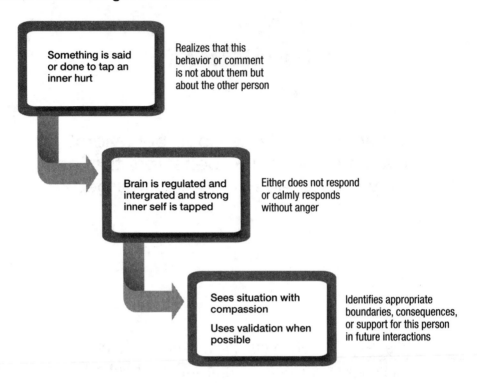

Something is said or done to tap an inner hurt	Realizes that this behavior or comment is not about them but about the other person
Brain is regulated and intergrated and strong inner self is tapped	Either does not respond or calmly responds without anger
Sees situation with compassion Uses validation when possible	Identifies appropriate boundaries, consequences, or support for this person in future interactions

In the following story from my own life, I was able to help my son, Tom, turn his dislike of a teacher into an opportunity to develop a strong inner self. (Note that this is the only story where I am *not* changing the name to protect identity. Sorry, Tom!)

A story: Validation builds self-compassion

Tom, my son, was in the fourth-grade gifted class. He came home from school one day crying.

I asked him, "What is wrong?"

He said, "I am so stupid."

I said, "How is that?"

He said, "I know a faster way to do this math problem, but the teacher said that I could not do it that way, that I had to do it his way."

I said, "How did that make you feel stupid?"

He said, "Because I could not get the teacher to understand that it was faster this way." *(His interpretation of the event led to this conclusion.)*

What is the inner hurt here? Tom felt rejected, unimportant, disregarded.

I said, "Tom, you are smarter than he is. You know two ways to do it, and he only knows one." *I wanted to validate Tom's value and worthiness.*

He said, "That is not possible. He has a college degree and I don't."

I said, "The teacher is better educated than you are, but you are smarter than he is. You know two ways to do the problem." *This was my validation of an inner strength.* "It doesn't hurt you to do it his way. All of your life you will meet people who have more authority than you do but who are not as smart as you are." *I wanted to provide this frame of reference so he does not misinterpret a similar event in the future.* "In this particular situation, the teacher is unable to be flexible. But you can be flexible. It doesn't harm you." *I wanted to validate equality, flexibility.*

This conversation *gave Tom self-compassion.* He understood that he—as a person—was fine and strong. He was valued, worthy, and flexible. While the situation was not to his liking, it did not impact his value as a person.

In this case, I did not ask my son to identify the teacher's thinking. I could have asked him, "Do you think that the teacher felt it might confuse other students if he let you do it your way? Do you think that he was afraid that you thought he was not a good teacher?"

It also would have been very easy for me to shame Tom. Humiliation occurs when criticism is added to the shame. I could have said, "How awful of you to criticize the teacher! You are to be respectful of adults. Shame on you." Or I could have said, "Why are you crying about that? That is so stupid to cry about that. You must be stupid if you cry about something that silly!"

All that would have done is reinforce an inner hurt. It would not have motivated good behavior or built a strong inner self.

Motivating good behaviors

To create good behaviors, there is a process called validation that was identified in the story above. The following protocol lists the steps for validating a person.

What is the protocol for validation?

Validation

- Calm the student.
- Help identify the deep hurt.
- Help identify the ways in which the deep hurt is not true.
- Visit the thinking of the other person involved.
- Identify the deep value/strengths that the student has.
- Identify the consequences for the behavior.
- Examine other choices for the future.

When the behavior must be managed because it cannot be changed

There are also situations where the behavior cannot be changed but must instead be managed. For example, one might have a student who is autistic.

In situations where the behavior must be managed, it is important to note that a process must be in place for constant monitoring of that student and adaptation of the interventions.

It is the same process used for triage, but you do 100% of these students, not 50% as you did for each group in the triage process.

Keep consequences in place; change the approach.

What does this mean in the classroom?

1. The emphasis of discipline should be on the *motivation* of good behaviors, which is the development of inner strength.

2. Vocabulary for naming emotions should *always* be provided in any discipline intervention.

3. Educators should identify their own emotional triggers.

4. The campus needs to use triage as a way to monitor the safety of everyone on the campus.

Managing Your Life

How do I keep my emotional stability as an educator?

First of all, Jordan Peterson has a wonderful quote: 'Don't compare yourself to others. Compare yourself to who you were yesterday.'[130]

To have fewer *negative* emotional responses in your life, it is necessary to have the following tools:

1. A future story and goals.

2. Management of time.

3. Management of money.

4. Management of self-talk (the back door). Understand that another's behavior is rarely about you. It is about them. Victor Frankl said that you cannot control what happens to you, but you can control how you interpret it.

5. Management of your expectations of others.

6. Key relationships of support and respect.

It helps significantly to have:

1. Spiritual resources (highly correlated to emotional stability and resilience).

2. Physical exercise.

3. Meditation/mindfulness/prayer.

4. Constant sources of new learning—to keep motivated, interested, and hopeful… in other words, to feel alive!

5. Daily gratitude.

Let's investigate those tools in more depth.

Future story and goals

Designing your life is more important than designing your career.

There are many ways to create your future story and set goals. One of the best systems out there is the FranklinCovey system of time management and goal setting. It does not really matter which system you use, as long as you use one consistently. Another favorite tool of mine for creating a future story is a "mind movie." You make your own movie about what you want your life to be.[131]

The point is this: A person is 95% likely to achieve their future story or meet their goals if the goals are in writing. You are only 7% likely to achieve your goals if you do not put them in writing.

1. Write down what your unique gifts are. What is it that you do well that is unique to you? Those gifts become the meaning in your life. Write down what your meaning is in life. Purpose is when you share those gifts with others. What is the purpose of your life? That is, how will you share those gifts? As a business? As a hobby? As a charitable endeavor? As a career?

2. Get a future story. A future story is a lot more than what your career is. It is for your life and includes relationships, purpose, meaning, money, career, hobbies, fun, etc. This is an example of the visual story board discussed earlier in the book, which is one way to do a future story:

Visual story board

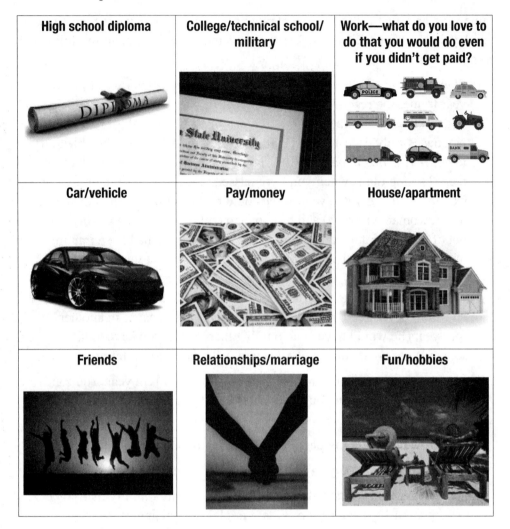

High school diploma	College/technical school/military	Work—what do you love to do that you would do even if you didn't get paid?
Car/vehicle	Pay/money	House/apartment
Friends	Relationships/marriage	Fun/hobbies

I redo my future story every year at the beginning of the year. I find it is absolutely important to revise it every five years because who you are as a person changes, you accomplish some of your goals and others are no longer important to you, you have new interests and life challenges, etc. It is a constantly adaptive environment.

Time management

Time is an area that I find few people manage well. They manage their time for the day, but not for their lives. Time management needs to have the following components:

1. Planning your life by decades. For example, I have planned out in five-year frames the rest of my life (yes, it is true!) and what I want to be able to do in those time frames. Does it mean that I will get all of that done? Not necessarily. It just means that these are things I want to be able to try to do. *Why is this important? Because people "age out."* What does that mean? Aging out is when you have passed the age to do something. For example, when my dad was 90, he could no longer drive. He had aged out. A woman who is 50 and has not had children yet has probably aged out of having biological children. I knew a man who had been training to be a boxer on the U.S. Olympic team. In a year that the U.S. did not participate in the Olympics because of a political protest, he was already one of the oldest members of the boxing team. He told me that he knew he would never get to participate in the Olympics because in another four years he would have aged out. In other words, you have to have some idea of what you want to make time to do in your lifetime.

2. Planning for three years, and particularly for the current year. You can develop goals for both your personal life and your career. I do this once a year and answer these questions:

   a. How do I want my personal life to look in one year? In three years?

   b. How do I want my career to look in one year? In three years?

   c. What are my personal goals for finances, health, family/marriage/ relationships, education/skills, fun/play/socializing, spiritual development, and character development for the coming year? Character goals are how you want to be a better person. Jordan Peterson states that *you should not compare yourself to others, but rather to who you were yesterday.*

   d. Out of these goals, what are my 90-day goals?

   e. Steven Covey says that you should take these time goals and break them down into months, then into weeks, and then into days.

3. For a week, use this time sheet and break down how you are spending your
time every day, every hour.

Sunday	Monday	Tuesday	Wednesday	Thursday	Friday	Saturday

If you keep track of your time for a week, you will recognize how much time
you actually "waste." For productive people, time is their most valuable
commodity.

4. Based upon what you know about your time, how will you reallocate it to
have more of what you want?

Money management

Most people are comfortable with the concept of a budget, but they do not make their budgets *based upon a realistic assessment of their emotional realities.*

If you are having difficulty with a budget, start out with an envelope system and cash. Do this for a month, or use play money to represent your real money. Glue six envelopes to a manila folder. Write on the outside of the envelope what the money spent in each area is, e.g., "rent/mortgage" (includes utilities), "transportation" (gas, car loan, repairs), "food/household," "tithe/savings," "childcare," "healthcare."

Simplest method: Go backward with your money. Write down what your gross pay is, what is deducted, and what your take-home pay is.

Write your take-home pay at the top of the page. Now start subtracting. Subtract your rent/mortgage, then subtract food, then subtract transportation, etc. If you have more bills left than money, you need to look to adjust amounts. If you have more money left than bills, figure out how you will invest/save/tithe it.

Now look at your envelopes. What are you actually spending? What can be adjusted?

Because everyone wants to belong and have friends and fun, emotional realities often dictate how money is spent. For example, I have a friend who loves boats and fishing. It is an emotional reality for him. He knows that it will take up a disproportionate amount of his budget. What are your emotional realities? What will you spend money on?

Identify in your budget your emotional realities. Can you afford them?

Key question: What are your long-term goals for your money?

There are much more sophisticated tools for managing your money than this. There are spreadsheets and apps devoted to budgeting and bookkeeping. The issue is, do you have any system at all for managing your money?

Manage your self-talk

Your self-talk is that back door you have into your brain that conveys negative messages and doubt. It might say things like:

1. This is stupid. This will never happen. Why try?

2. Remember those last three failures you had? Why would this one be any different?

3. You will never be as good as she is. Why try?

4. You don't have enough time. You don't have enough money.

How do you manage that self-talk? Here are some questions to ask yourself:

1. What is the worst thing that could happen if this does not work out? Will you be exactly where you are right now?

2. What will people say about me? (That is their problem, not yours.)

3. Is that actually true? Identify two times when it was not true.

4. Will it make a difference in five years?

5. Who will probably support me in this venture?

6. Will I stagnate even more if I do not do this? Will I lose a part of myself if I do not try this?

Manage your expectations of others and your boundaries

Whenever you hear the words *should, ought, could have,* etc., you have identified an expectation you have for someone else or for yourself. I realized that one of the phrases that was repeated in my head was: *You should have known better.* As I started to think about that, I thought: *Really?* How would I have known that this is an accounting error? How would I know that this is a marketing issue? I am not an accountant or a marketer. Each person only has so much time to know so much.

That voice that says I should have known better is a voice I have determined to delete from the inside of my head. It is just not possible to know everything. In managing this expectation of myself, I'm also managing my self-talk as discussed above.

Expectations show up a lot in romantic relationships and in relationships with colleagues. Examine those messages in your head. Are they really true?

Boundaries are the lines that you do not allow to be crossed in your life. One of the best books on boundaries is *Boundaries Updated and Expanded Edition: When to Say Yes, How to Say No to Take Control of Your Life* by Henry Cloud and John Townsend.

If boundaries are an issue in your life, I recommend this book to you. You know you have a boundary problem if you cannot say no.

Identify key relationships of support

One of the activities that I recommend you do is draw a circle on a piece of paper and put your name in it. Then draw circles around that circle with the names of people who are important to you.

You can have as many circles as you want. If a person will support you in doing what you want to do, then draw a solid line to that person. If a person will support you some of the time and not support you other times, then draw a dotted line. If a person will never support you, then draw no line. Make a plan about how you will deal with the person who will not support you. Otherwise you will allow yourself to be derailed.

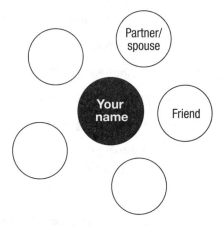

As I mentioned previously, it also helps significantly to have:

   a. Spiritual resources (highly correlated to emotional stability and resilience)

   b. Physical exercise

   c. Meditation/mindfulness/prayer

   d. Constant sources of new learning—to keep motivated, interested, and hopeful … in other words, to feel alive!

   e. Daily gratitude (lowers cortisol levels in the body by 25%)

Particularly in the U.S., there is a lot of conversation about managing careers and businesses, but virtually nothing is said about managing your emotional life.

Not everything in life can be managed according to a schedule. Examples include illness, death, disaster, job loss, etc. But having a plan for your life can keep emotional destabilizers from destroying you. An unexpected event may cause delay, it may temporarily halt the plan, but the possibility of being destroyed by the event is significantly less if you have a plan in place.

It is the management of your life that brings emotional stability, that brings satisfaction and happiness. If you want to create emotional wealth for yourself and your students—instead of emotional poverty—have a plan. It keeps everything else in perspective.

What We Can Do

What does all of this mean for my classroom and for my life?

Given the research findings, we know it is possible to develop emotional competence and strength in students.

We can teach students about a regulated, integrated brain and how to calm themselves.

We can help build strong inner selves in students through validation.

We can construct classrooms in which the emotional noise is lessened.

We can create safer classrooms and campuses by promoting fewer "less than" and "separate from" experiences for students.

We can triage our student populations to better address emotional issues, just as we do for academic issues.

We can be aware of our own emotional realities and our participation in the safety and well-being of students and the campus.

We will always keep consequences in place, but we can change the approach.

Education has always been and will always be a human endeavor, a social interaction. By paying more attention to the emotional well-being of our students and ourselves, we ensure a high-quality education that is safe—not dangerous—for students in every demographic.

Endnotes

[1] United States Secret Service & United States Department of Education, "The Final Report and Findings of the Safe School Initiative"

[2] D. Siegel, *Mindsight*

[3] *Ibid.*, page 18

[4] *Ibid.*, pages 18–19

[5] *Ibid.*, page 19

[6] M. M. Kishiyama et al., "Socioeconomic Disparities Affect Prefrontal Function in Children"

[7] D. Siegel, *Mindsight,* page 26

[8] S. Stosny, *The Powerful Self,* page 71

[9] D. Siegel, *Mindsight,* page 26

[10] R. Callahan & R. Trubo, *Tapping the Healer Within;* A. Ortney, *Gorilla Thumps and Bear Hugs*

[11] "Core Self-Evaluations"

[12] S. Stosny, *Treating Attachment Abuse,* page 18

[13] S. Stosny, *Soar Above,* page 4

[14] E. Erikson, *A Way of Looking at Things,* page 609

[15] E. Erikson, *Identity: Youth and Crisis,* page 97

[16] S. Scheck, "The Stages of Psychosocial Development According to Erik H. Erikson"

[17] E. Erikson, *Identity and the Life Cycle,* page 154

[18] *Ibid.*

[19] S. Scheck, "The Stages of Psychosocial Development According to Erik H. Erikson"

[20] *Ibid.*

[21] *Ibid.*

[22] *Ibid.*

[23] E. Erikson, *Identity: Youth and Crisis,* page 136

[24] K. S. Berger, *The Developing Person Through the Life Span*

[25] D. Elkind, "Egocentrism in Adolescence"

[26] K. S. Berger, *The Developing Person Through the Life Span,* page 409

[27] E. Erikson, *Identity: Youth and Crisis*

[28] E. Oberle & K. A. Schonert-Reichl, "Relations Among Peer Acceptance, Inhibitory Control, and Math Achievement in Early Adolescence," page 45, emphasis added

[29] K. S. Berger, *The Developing Person Through the Life Span,* page 443

[30] *Ibid.*, page 445

[31] J. Bowlby, *Attachment: Attachment and Loss (Vol. 1)*

[32] C. Mooney, *Theories of Attachment,* page 17

[33] M. D. Ainsworth & S. M. Bell, "Attachment, Exploration, and Separation: Illustrated by the Behavior of One-Year-Olds in a Strange Situation"

[34] S. Stosny, *Treating Attachment Abuse,* page 21

[35] *Ibid.*, page 22

[36] *Ibid.*

[37] *Ibid.*

[38] *Ibid.*, page 61

[39] J. Peterson, *12 Rules for Life,* page 147

[40] D. Siegel, *Mindsight*

[41] *Ibid.*

[42] *Ibid.*

[43] *Ibid.*, page 171, emphasis added

[44] B. H. Tucker, "Teach Teddy"

[45] R. K. Payne, *Working with Students*

[46] R. K. Payne, *A Framework for Understanding Poverty*

[47] *Ibid.*

[48] R. K. Payne & B. H. Tucker, *Research-Based Strategies*

[49] C. Mooney, *Theories of Attachment*

[50] S. Stosny, *Treating Attachment Abuse*, page 52

[51] *Ibid.*, pages 50–51

[52] *Ibid.*

[53] B. Denizet-Lewis, "Why Are More American Teenagers Than Ever Suffering from Severe Anxiety?"

[54] S. Stosny, *Treating Attachment Abuse*

[55] S. Stosny, *The Powerful Self*

[56] T. Pearce, "Popular Kids More Likely to Be Bullies, Study Finds"

[57] S. Attkisson, *The Smear*

[58] R. K. Payne, "What Information Does *A Framework for Understanding Poverty* Have That Cannot Be Obtained Easily from Other Sources?"

[59] J. Peterson, *12 Rules for Life,* page 319

[60] S. Stosny, *Treating Attachment Abuse,* pages 92–93, emphasis added

[61] S. Akhtar & H. Parens, *Revenge*, location 118

[62] J. Singal, "Here's the Biggest Study Yet on the Differences Between Male and Female Brains"

[63] G. L. Jantz, "Brain Differences Between Genders"

[64] J. Singal, "Here's the Biggest Study Yet on the Differences Between Male and Female Brains"

[65] *Ibid.*

[66] G. L. Jantz, "Brain Differences Between Genders"

[67] *Ibid.*

[68] C. Bergland, "Scientists Identify Why Girls Often Mature Faster Than Boys"; A. Sifferlin, "Why Girls' Brains Mature Faster Than Boys' Brains"; M. Gurian et al., *Boys and Girls Learn Differently!*

[69] M. Gurian et al., *Boys and Girls Learn Differently!;* L. Sax, *Why Gender Matters*

[70] O. Khazan, "Male and Female Brains Really Are Built Differently"

[71] M. Gurian et al., *Boys and Girls Learn Differently!;* O. Khazan, "Male and Female Brains Really Are Built Differently"; M. Cohut, "How Different Are Men's and Women's Brains?"

[72] M. Gurian et al., *Boys and Girls Learn Differently!;* M. Gurian & K. Stevens, "With Boys and Girls in Mind"; G. Gross, "How Boys and Girls Learn Differently"

[73] M. Gurian et al., *Boys and Girls Learn Differently!;* L. Sax, *Why Gender Matters*

[74] M. Gurian et al., *Boys and Girls Learn Differently!*

[75] L. Sax, *Why Gender Matters*

[76] M. Gurian et al., *Boys and Girls Learn Differently!;* L. Sax, *Why Gender Matters*

[77] *Ibid.*

[78] S. H. Bolling, "The Differences in the Gross Motor Development of Boys and Girls in Early Childhood"; P. Moreno-Briseño, "Sex-Related Differences in Motor Learning and Performance"

[79] *Ibid.*

[80] L. Sax, *Why Gender Matters*

[81] M. Gurian et al., *Boys and Girls Learn Differently!*

[82] L. Sax, *Why Gender Matters*

[83] *Ibid.*

[84] *Ibid.*

[85] M. Gurian et al., *Boys and Girls Learn Differently!;* L. Sax, *Why Gender Matters*

[86] L. Sax, *Why Gender Matters*

[87] M. Gurian et al., *Boys and Girls Learn Differently!;* L. Sax, *Why Gender Matters*

[88] L. Sax, *Why Gender Matters*

[89] *Ibid.*

[90] *Ibid.*

[91] M. Gurian et al., *Boys and Girls Learn Differently!*; R. Wiseman, *Masterminds and Wingmen*

[92] L. Sax, *Why Gender Matters*

[93] *Ibid.*

[94] *Ibid.*

[95] J. Peterson, *12 Rules for Life,* pages 330–331

[96] V. Satir, *Peoplemaking*

[97] G. Sheehy, *Passages: Predictable Crises of Adult Life,* page 30

[98] *Ibid.,* page 31

[99] *Ibid.,* pages 331–332

[100] *Ibid.,* page 144

[101] *Ibid.,* page 185

[102] *Ibid.,* page 199

[103] *Ibid.,* page 197

[104] *Ibid.,* page 246

[105] *Ibid.,* page 348

[106] *Ibid.,* page 349

[107] *Ibid.,* page 358

[108] *Ibid.,* page 46

[109] *Ibid.,* page 168

[110] *Ibid.,* page 365–366

[111] *Ibid.,* page 368

[112] Note that this is based on statistics about machinists, but similar trends exist in many professions; J. Schleckser, "If You Work with Your Mind, There's No Retirement for You"; A. Brenoff, "Early Retirement May Be the Kiss of Death, Study Finds"

[113] G. Sheehy, *Passages: Predictable Crises of Adult Life,* p. 484

[114] K. S. Berger, *The Developing Person Through the Life Span*

[115] J. Peterson, *12 Rules for Life,* page 122

[116] C. Taylor, "70% of Rich Families Lose Their Wealth by the Second Generation"

[117] B. Denizet-Lewis, "Why Are More American Teenagers Than Ever Suffering from Severe Anxiety?"

[118] C. A. Childress, *An Attachment-Based Model of Parental Alienation*

[119] M. Kismet, "Psychological Effects of Growing up Without a Father"

[120] P. Tough, *How Children Succeed*

[121] *Ibid.*

[122] O. F. Kernberg, *Borderline Conditions and Pathological Narcissism,* page 229

[123] American Psychiatric Association, *Diagnostic and Statistical Manual of Mental Disorders* (5th ed.)

[124] E. L. Zuckerman, *Clinician's Thesaurus: The Guide to Conducting Interviews and Writing Psychological Reports*

[125] V. L. Dunckley, "Gray Matters: Too Much Screen Time Damages the Brain"

[126] *Ibid.*

[127] J. Bloom, "God, Religion, and America's Addiction Crisis"

[128] J. Guynn, "Just Say No to Addicting Kids to Technology, Former Facebook, Google Employees, Investors Urge"

[129] V. Satir, *Peoplemaking*

[130] J. Peterson, *12 Rules for Life*

[131] Mind Movies, "Homepage"

Appendix A
Study Guide

Emotional Poverty review questions

Introduction

1. What is the four-part definition of emotional poverty?

2. How does emotional poverty impact all economic groups, particularly affluent populations?

3. How is school safety related to this four-part definition?

4. What does the statement "consequences will always be needed; it is the approach that needs to change" mean?

5. Ninety percent of school discipline issues come from 10–15% of the students. Think of a student you taught who falls into that 10–15%. Please fill out the checklist for identifying emotional resources in the Introduction for that student. After you filled out the checklist, what did you learn about that student's emotional resources?

Chapter 1

1. Can you teach the hand model of the brain, a powerful mental model, to your class? Why would you do that? What is the benefit for the students?

2. Which parts of the brain have the most influence in determining and controlling an emotional meltdown?

3. What is the definition of an emotional meltdown?

4. Stosny says "emotion is processed 200–5,000 times faster than thought." Why is that information beneficial to know?

5. Compare and contrast calming techniques that you currently use with those that are suggested in Chapter 1. Which techniques are you willing to try?

Chapter 2

1. Brain development of the emotional self occurs from birth to three and again during adolescence, when the brain prunes and rewires itself. How is that process the same, and how is it different at those two times?

2. What is the role of self-construction?

3. How does Erikson's research on child development explain behaviors that you may see in the classroom?

4. Can you give examples of students who exhibit a difference between their emotional age and their chronological age?

5. Explain the difference between a weak inner self and a strong inner self.

6. How does adolescence shape a student's identity?

7. What is the difference between psychological control and behavioral control? Why is psychological control so damaging for adolescents?

8. How can a weak inner self lead to bad behavior? Why do many of the discipline techniques used in school actually increase bad behavior?

Chapter 3

1. What is bonding and attachment? How does it influence students' and teachers' interactions in the classroom?

2. Compare and contrast the significant attributes of the four attachment and bonding styles.

3. What discipline strategies have you used to address each of the bonding and attachment styles? Evaluate your results.

4. Identify which tools and strategies from Chapter 3 you will use when there is a bonding and attachment issue that needs to be addressed.

Chapter 4

1. What is the impact of the repeated process of bonding, then separation, then individuation, and then new bonding on children and adults?

2. How does anger benefit the inner self?

3. Identify the significant impact anger, anxiety, and avoidance have on students.

4. What can you do to help an angry, anxious, or avoidant student or colleague?

5. Identify the differences between shame, humiliation, and guilt.

6. Examine the impact that feeling 'less than' or 'separate from' has on students and adults throughout their lives.

7. Explain how you had to deal with issues that created shame, humiliation, and/or guilt in and out of the classroom.

8. How can you reduce comments that tend to increase shame, humiliation, and/or guilt and increase comments that tend to help develop a strong inner self?

9. Evaluate how bullying has impacted you personally and how it has affected your students. How did you deal with both?

10. How does resentment impact your classroom? What can you do to reduce the impact?

11. Will your campus use the emotional triage process? How will that process keep students and staff safer?

Chapter 5

1. Why is there such concern over addressing issues related to gender differences?

2. Using the female/male tendencies or patterns chart in Chapter 5, evaluate the tendencies or patterns. Do they reflect your life experiences?

3. Why do many males have difficulty verbalizing emotions?

4. Why do males often need more time to process emotions?

5. How will you change your discipline approaches for more effectiveness with males?

Chapter 6

1. Who might the students and teacher bring with them to class every day? How might this impact what happens in the classroom?

2. What is the emotional dance that takes place in classrooms every day?

3. Compare and contrast emotional noise that is low and high. What are the attributes that create noise?

4. What are the issues, from the adult perspective, that impact the emotional dance in the classroom?

5. How does the bonding and attachment style of the student and the educator influence the emotional dance in the classroom?

6. Explain how a student's or educator's core inner hurts create emotional triggers.

7. How does the ebb and flow of the energy in our lifetime impact our ability to deal with stress? How does it impact classroom management?

8. How do the stages of adult development impact the emotional noise in the classroom?

9. Of the seven factors in adult development that are lifelong, which of those are most impacting you right now?

Chapter 7

1. Why is family function more critical for student success than family structure?

2. How might screen addictions, affluence, fatherless households, and adult addiction impact a "less than" and "separate from" external environment?

3. How might examining the results of the adverse childhood experiences (ACE) questionnaire benefit you in the classroom?

4. Why are students and parents with mental illness, biochemical issues, and/or personality disorders so challenging to work with in the classroom?

Chapter 8

1. What motivates good behavior?

2. What is the process of validation? Can you give an example of how you went through that process with a student?

3. If you can't change a student's behavior, how do you manage it?

Chapter 9

1. Examine the tools or strategies you currently use to reduce your own negative emotional responses to events in your life. How are they improving your life?

2. Which of the management strategies and tools from Chapter 9 will you adapt to help your emotional stability?

Chapter 10

1. What do you consider to be the essential knowledge gained from this book that will enable you to help students succeed?

2. What do you consider to be the essential knowledge gained from this book that will enable *you* to succeed?

3. Of the statements in Chapter 10 of all the things we can do, with which ones of those do you most agree?

Appendix B
Classroom Management/ Procedures Checklist

According to Herbert Walberg (1990), up to 65% of achievement can be attributed to classroom management. Ninety-five percent of discipline referrals come during the first or last five minutes of class because of the lack of procedures.

Procedures checklist

The following checklist is adapted from "Guidelines for the First Days of School" from the Research Development Center for Teacher Education, Research on Classrooms, University of Texas, Austin.

Starting class	My procedure
Taking attendance	
Marking absences	
Tardy students	
Giving makeup work for absentees	
Enrolling new students	
Un-enrolling students	
Students who have to leave school early	
Warm-up activity (that students begin as soon as they walk into classroom)	

(continued on next page)

(continued from previous page)

Instructional time	My procedure
Student movement within classroom	
Use of cellphones and headphones	
Student movement in and out of classroom	
Going to restroom	
Getting students' attention	
Students talking during class	
What students do when their work is completed	
Working together as group(s)	
Handing in papers/homework	
Appropriate headings for papers	
Bringing/distributing/using textbooks	
Leaving room for special class	
Students who don't have paper and/or pencils	
Signal(s) for getting student attention	
Touching other students in classroom	
Eating food in classroom	
Laboratory procedures (materials and supplies, safety routines, cleaning up)	
Students who get sick during class	
Using pencil sharpener	
Listing assignments/homework/due dates	
Systematically monitoring student learning during instruction	

Ending class	My procedure
Putting things away	
Dismissing class	
Collecting papers and assignments	

(continued on next page)

(continued from previous page)

Other	My procedure
Lining up for lunch/recess/special events	
Walking to lunch/recess	
Putting away coats and backpacks	
Cleaning out locker	
Preparing for fire drills and/or bomb threats	
Going to gym for assemblies/pep rallies	
Respecting teacher's desk and storage areas	
Appropriately handling/using computers/equipment	

Student accountability	My procedure
Late work	
Missing work	
Extra credit	
Redoing work and/or retaking tests	
Incomplete work	
Neatness	
Papers with no names	
Using pens, pencils, colored markers	
Using computer-generated products	
Internet access on computers	
Setting and assigning due dates	
Writing on back of paper	
Makeup work and amount of time for makeup work	
Use of mobile devices, headphones during class	
Letting students know assignments missed during absence	
Percentage of grade for major tests, homework, etc.	

(continued on next page)

(continued from previous page)

Student accountability	My procedure
Explaining your grading policy	
Letting new students know your procedures	
Having contact with all students at least once during week	
Exchanging papers	
Using Internet for posting assignments and sending them in	

How will you ...	My procedure
Determine grades on report cards (components and weights of those components)?	
Grade daily assignments?	
Record grades so that assignments and dates are included?	
Have students keep records of their own grades?	
Make sure your assignments and grading reflect progress against standards?	
Notify parents when students are not passing or having other academic problems?	
Contact parents if a problem arises regarding student behavior?	
Keep records and documentation of student behavior?	
Document adherence to IEP (individualized education plan)?	
Return graded papers in a timely manner?	
Monitor students who have serious health issues (peanut allergies, diabetes, epilepsy, etc.)?	

Source: Adapted from "Guidelines for the First Days of School," Research Development Center for Teacher Education, Research on Classrooms, University of Texas, Austin.

Appendix C
Federal and State Policies that Increase Emotional Poverty in Students

This book has focused on the emotional realities that schools attempt to address. There is also a larger frame of government policy that helps create emotional poverty in students.

These government policy issues include, but are not limited to, the following:

1. The segregation of public schooling by race/ethnicity and financial poverty. This creates a "less than" and "separate from" experience.

2. Policies that devote resources to those who can vote versus those who cannot vote—i.e., children. "The demographer Samuel Preston warned in 1984 that the United States had made 'a set of private and public choices that have dramatically altered the age profile of well-being' by devoting resources toward improving conditions for the elderly while neglecting to do the same for families with children. 'The constituency for children in public decisions simply appears too feeble to fight back,' he wrote" (Gibson-Davis & Percheski, 2018).

3. A federal education system that punishes young children for failure to learn at a given pace (grade retention and testing policies that retain young children for as many as three years). The research is so clear about the relationship between fear-based learning practices and a weak inner self. (See Chapter 2.)

4. The elimination of play and arts from daily schooling—no recess, no arts, no music. Children make sense of their reality through play. Adults use play to escape reality. This is an adult understanding that is not true for children. This lack of opportunities to make sense out of reality through art and play leads to less emotional development.

5. The high rate of denial of welfare benefits to two-parent households means that young males from poverty often grow up in fatherless households—which has a huge influence on the inner development of a young male. (See Chapter 7.)

6. Curriculum standards that ignore the roles of emotion and relationships in learning. Emotion and cognition are double coded (Greenspan & Benderly, 1997).

7. Policies and practices that limit healthcare access, particularly in rural areas, for children who are in financial poverty. Dental care and healthcare are key factors in emotional well-being.

8. Policies and legislation that limit affordable housing. For many families, the lack of affordable housing leads to increased student mobility, which often significantly decreases emotional development and learning.

9. In the 1970s the following three courses were dropped from most high school curricula: Home and Family Living, Food and Nutrition, and Personal Finance. Lack of knowledge in these three areas can create the greatest amount of emotional poverty. The idea that students should learn how to manage their lives was dropped in favor of students learning how to manage their careers. These life-skills courses need to be reinstated. You cannot teach or practice what you do not know.

10. In some states, child abuse and neglect laws are resulting in overzealous parenting. In Maryland, a child cannot be left alone for any amount of time until age eight. In Illinois the age is 14 (for a vaguely worded, "unreasonable" amount of time). On the other hand, Utah just passed a "free range" law for children that redefines neglect to exclude things like letting a child go to a park or walk to a nearby store alone. A 2007 study looked at parenting and its impact on the development of anxiety in children. "Granting autonomy" was the parent behavior most involved in reducing anxiety. As you know from this book, autonomy is a developmental stage that begins around age two and helps develop a strong inner self. The research does note that genetics also play a strong role in anxiety (Petersen, 2018).

Appendix C References

Gibson-Davis, C., & Percheski, C. (2018, May 18). Why the wealth gap hits families the hardest. *New York Times.* Retrieved from https://www.nytimes.com/2018/05/18/opinion/wealth-inequality-families-children-elderly.html

Greenspan, S. I., & Benderly, B. L. (1997). *The growth of the mind and the endangered origins of intelligence.* Reading, MA: Addison-Wesley.

Petersen, A. (2018, June 1). The overprotected American child. *Wall Street Journal.* Retrieved from https://www.wsj.com/articles/the-overprotected-american-child-1527865038

Bibliography

Ainsworth, M. D., & Bell, S. M. (1970). Attachment, exploration, and separation: Illustrated by the behavior of one-year-olds in a strange situation. *Child Development, 41*(1), 49–67. doi:10.2307/1127388

Akhtar, S., & Parens, H. (Eds.). (2013). *Revenge: Narcissistic injury, rage, and retaliation* [Kindle ed.]. Lanham, MD: Jason Aronson.

American Psychiatric Association. (2013). *Diagnostic and statistical manual of mental disorders* (5th ed.). Arlington, VA: American Psychiatric Publishing.

Attkisson, S. (2017). *The smear: How shady political operatives and fake news control what you see, what you think, and how you vote.* New York, NY: Harper.

Berger, K. S. (2011). *The developing person through the life span* (8th ed.). New York, NY: Worth.

Bergland, C. (2013, December 20). Scientists identify why girls often mature faster than boys. Retrieved from https://www.psychologytoday.com/us/blog/the-athletes-way/201312/scientists-identify-why-girls-often-mature-faster-boys

Bloom, J. (2017, August 7). God, religion, and America's addiction crisis. Retrieved from https://mosaicmagazine.com/essay/2017/08/god-religion-and-americas-addiction-crisis/

Bolling, S. H. (2017, September 26). The differences in the gross motor development of boys and girls in early childhood. Retrieved from https://howtoadult.com/differences-gross-motor-development-boys-girls-early-childhood-18177.html

Bowlby, J. (1969). *Attachment: Attachment and loss* (vol. 1). New York, NY: Basic Books.

Brenoff, A. (2016, April 28). Early retirement may be the kiss of death, study finds. Retrieved from https://www.huffingtonpost.com/entry/early-retirement-may-be-the-kiss-of-death-study-finds_us_57221aa3e4b01a5ebde49eff

Brown, S. L. (2017, May 16). Adult children of abusive parents—when parents are pathological. Retrieved from http://saferelationshipsmagazine.com/adult-children-abusive-parents-parents-pathological

Callahan, R., & Trubo, R. (2002). *Tapping the healer within: Using thought-field therapy to instantly conquer your fears, anxieties, and emotional distress.* New York, NY: McGraw-Hill Education.

Childress, C. A. (2015). *An attachment-based model of parental alienation: Foundations.* Pasadena, CA: Oaksong.

Cloud, H., & Townsend, J. (1992). *Boundaries updated and expanded edition: When to say yes, how to say no to take control of your life.* Grand Rapids, MI: Zondervan.

Cohut, M. (2017, September 29). How different are men's and women's brains? Retrieved from https://www.medicalnewstoday.com/articles/319592.php

Core self-evaluations. (2018). Retrieved from https://en.wikipedia.org/wiki/Core_self-evaluations

Denizet-Lewis, B. (2017, October 11). Why are more American teenagers than ever suffering from severe anxiety? *The New York Times Magazine.* Retrieved from https://www.nytimes.com/2017/10/11/magazine/why-are-more-american-teenagers-than-ever-suffering-from-severe-anxiety.html

Dunckley, V. L. (2014, February 27). Gray matters: Too much screen time damages the brain. Retrieved from https://www.psychologytoday.com/us/blog/mental-wealth/201402/gray-matters-too-much-screen-time-damages-the-brain

Dunphy, D. (1963). The social structure of urban adolescent peer groups. *Sociometry, 26,* 230–246.

Elkind, D. (1967). Egocentrism in adolescence. *Child Development, 38,* 1025–1034.

Erikson, E. (1968). *Identity: Youth and crisis.* New York, NY: Norton. Retrieved from https://archive.org/stream/300656427ErikHEriksonIdentityYouthAndCrisis1WWNortonCompany1968/300656427-Erik-H-Erikson-Identity-Youth-and-Crisis-1-W-W-Norton-Company-1968_djvu.txt

Erikson, E. (1980). *Identity and the life cycle.* New York, NY: Norton.

Erikson, E. (1987). *A way of looking at things: Selected papers from 1930 to 1980.* New York, NY: Norton.

Gender Spectrum. (2017). Understanding gender. Retrieved from https://www.genderspectrum.org/quick-links/understanding-gender/

Gross, G. (2014, July 16). How boys and girls learn differently. Retrieved from https://www.huffingtonpost.com/dr-gail-gross/how-boys-and-girls-learn-differently_b_5339567.html

Gurian, M., Henley, P., & Trueman, T. (2001). *Boys and girls learn differently! A guide for teachers and parents*. San Francisco: Jossey-Bass/John Wiley.

Gurian, M., & Stevens, K. (2004). With boys and girls in mind. *Educational Leadership, 62*(3), 21–26. Retrieved from http://www.ascd.org/publications/educational-leadership/nov04/vol62/num03/With-Boys-and-Girls-in-Mind.aspx

Guynn, J. (2018, February 5). Just say no to addicting kids to technology, former Facebook, Google employees, investors urge. Retrieved from https://www.firstcoastnews.com/article/news/nation-now/just-say-no-to-addicting-kids-to-technology-former-facebook-google-employees-investors-urge/465-546e425e-a261-445e-9066-b42b00e57bb2

Hetherington, E. M., Parke, R. D., Gauvain, M., & Locke, V. O. (2004). *Child psychology: A contemporary viewpoint* (5th ed.). New York, NY: McGraw-Hill. Retrieved from http://highered.mheducation.com/sites/0072820144/student_view0/chapter15/index.html

Kernberg, O. F. (1975). *Borderline conditions and pathological narcissism*. New York, NY: Aronson.

Kishiyama, M. M., Boyce, W. T., Jimenez, A. M., Perry, L. M., & Knight, R. T. (2009). Socioeconomic disparities affect prefrontal function in children. *Journal of Cognitive Neuroscience, 21*(6), 1106–1115. doi:10.1162/jocn.2009.21101

Kismet, M. (2018, January 14). Psychological effects of growing up without a father. Retrieved from https://owlcation.com/social-sciences/Psychological-Effects-On-Men-Growing-Up-Without-A-Father

Kolata, G. (1995, February 28). Man's world, woman's world? Brain studies point to differences. *The New York Times*. Retrieved from https://www.nytimes.com/1995/02/28/science/man-s-world-woman-s-world-brain-studies-point-to-differences.html

Jantz, G. L. (2014, February 27). Brain differences between genders. Retrieved from https://www.psychologytoday.com/us/blog/hope-relationships/201402/brain-differences-between-genders

Khazan, O. (2013, December 2). Male and female brains really are built differently. Retrieved from https://www.theatlantic.com/health/archive/2013/12/male-and-female-brains-really-are-built-differently/281962/

Lambrozo, T. (2012, August 28). Explaining gender differences. Retrieved from https://www.psychologytoday.com/us/blog/explananda/201208/explaining-gender-differences

Lindell, A. K., & Kidd, E. (2011). Why right-brain teaching is half-witted: A critique of the misapplication of neuroscience to education. *Mind, Brain, and Education, 5*(3), 121–127.

Lumen Learning. (n.d.). Gender differences in the classroom. Retrieved from https://courses.lumenlearning.com/educationalpsychology/chapter/gender-differences-in-the-classroom/

Mind Movies. (2018). Homepage. Retrieved from https://www.mindmovies.com/

Mooney, C. G. (2009). *Theories of attachment: An introduction to Bowlby, Ainsworth, Gerber, Brazelton, Kennell, and Klaus.* St. Paul, MN: Redleaf Press.

Moreno-Briseño, P., Díaz, R., Campos-Romo, A., & Fernandez-Ruiz, J. (2010, December 23). Sex-related differences in motor learning and performance. *Behavioral and Brain Functions, 6,* 74. doi:10.1186/1744-9081-6-74

Oberle, E., & Schonert-Reichl, K. A. (2013). Relations among peer acceptance, inhibitory control, and math achievement in early adolescence. *Journal of Applied Developmental Psychology, 34*(1), 45–51.

Ortner, A. (2016). *Gorilla thumps and bear hugs: A tapping solution children's story.* Carlsbad, CA: Hay House.

Payne, R. K. (2006). *Working with students.* Highlands, TX: aha! Process.

Payne, R. K. (2008). *Under-resourced learners: Eight strategies to boost student achievement.* Highlands, TX: aha! Process.

Payne, R. K. (2009). What information does *A Framework for Understanding Poverty* have that cannot be obtained easily from other sources? Why do critics love to hate it and practitioners love to use it? Retrieved from https://www.ahaprocess.com/wp-content/uploads/2013/08/Framework-for-Understanding-Poverty-Info-Not-Easily-Obtained-Elsewhere.pdf

Payne, R. K. (2013). *A framework for understanding poverty* (5th rev. ed.). Highlands, TX: aha! Process.

Payne, R. K., & O'Neill-Baker, E. (2016). *How much of yourself do you own? A process for building your emotional resources* (rev. ed.). Highlands, TX: aha! Process.

Payne, R. K., & Tucker, B. H. (2017). *Research-based strategies: Narrowing the achievement gap for under-resourced students* (rev. ed.). Highlands, TX: aha! Process.

Pearce, T. (2011, February 8). Popular kids more likely to be bullies, study finds. Retrieved from https://www.theglobeandmail.com/life/parenting/popular-kids-more-likely-to-be-bullies-study-finds/article570489/

Peterson, J. (2018). *12 rules for life: An antidote to chaos.* Toronto, Canada: Random House of Canada.

Reid, R. (2018, January 29). Stop using the excuse that 'boys mature slower than girls' for bad behaviour. Retrieved from http://metro.co.uk/2018/01/29/stop-using-excuse-boys-mature-slower-girls-bad-behaviour-7270774/

Satir, V. (1972). *Peoplemaking.* Palo Alto, CA: Science and Behavior Books.

Sax, L. (2006). Six degrees of separation: What teachers need to know about the emerging science of sex differences. *Educational Horizons, 84*(3), 190–200.

Sax, L. (2010). *Girls on the edge.* New York, NY. Basic Books.

Sax, L. (2017). *Why gender matters: What parents and teachers need to know about the emerging science of sex differences* (2nd ed.). New York, NY. Harmony Books.

Scheck, S. (2005). The stages of psychosocial development according to Erik H. Erikson (excerpt). Retrieved from https://www.grin.com/document/284265

Schleckser, J. (2017, November 21). If you work with your mind, there's no retirement for you. https://www.inc.com/jim-schleckser/there-is-no-retirement-and-thats-a-good-thing.html

Sheehy, G. (1977). *Passages: Predictable crises of adult life.* New York, NY: Bantam.

Siegel, D. (2010). *Mindsight: The new science of personal transformation.* New York, NY: Bantam.

Sifferlin, A. (2013, December 19). Why girls' brains mature faster than boys' brains. *Time.* Retrieved from http://healthland.time.com/2013/12/19/why-girls-brains-mature-faster-than-boys-brains/

Singal, J. (2017, April 6). Here's the biggest study yet on the differences between male and female brains. Retrieved from https://www.thecut.com/2017/04/heres-the-biggest-study-yet-on-sex-based-brain-differences.html

Stosny, S. (1995). *Treating attachment abuse: A compassionate approach.* New York, NY: Springer.

Stosny, S. (2003). *The powerful self: A workbook for therapeutic self-empowerment.* Germantown, MD: CompassionPower.

Stosny, S. (2016). *Soar above: How to use the most profound part of your brain under any kind of stress.* Deerfield Beach, FL: Health Communications.

Taylor, C. (2015, June 17). 70% of rich families lose their wealth by the second generation. Retrieved from http://time.com/money/3925308/rich-families-lose-wealth/

Tough, P. (2013). *How children succeed: Grit, curiosity, and the hidden power of character.* Boston, MA: Mariner Books.

Tucker, B. H. (2014). Teach teddy. Retrieved from https://www.ahaprocess.com/wp-content/uploads/2015/02/Teddy.pdf

United States Secret Service, & United States Department of Education. (2004). The final report and findings of the Safe School Initiative. Retrieved from https://www2.ed.gov/admins/lead/safety/preventingattacksreport.pdf

Walberg, H. J. (1990). Productive teaching and instruction: Assessing the knowledge base. *Phi Delta Kappan,* February, 470–478.

Wiseman, R. (2013). *Masterminds and wingmen: Helping our boys cope with schoolyard power, locker-room tests, girlfriends, and the new rules of boy world.* New York, NY: Harmony Books.

Zuckerman, E. L. (2010). *Clinician's thesaurus: The guide to conducting interviews and writing psychological reports* (7th ed.). New York, NY: The Guilford Press.

Acknowledgments

I would like to thank so many people who helped make this book possible.

First, there were all the readers—people who took the time to read and comment on the drafts. Some of them even allowed their stories to be included in the book. To Bethanie Tucker, Jim Littlejohn, Ruben Perez, Chestin Auzenne-Curl, Michael Curl, Kirven Tillis, Kim Ellis, Karen Coffey, Galen Hoffstadt, Rickey Frierson, Rebecca Katz, Jack Moye, Cindy Kirby, Judy Weber, Roger Gallazzi, Pete Gleason, Gary Rudick, Haley Ford, Ellen Williams, Lynn Dodge, Rendy Belcher, Karen Barber, Vern Reed, Martinrex Kedziora, Jim Ott, Jennifer Hedinger, Sharon Ray, and Steve Johnson and his ESC VI staff members, I offer my heartfelt thanks for the insightful feedback, encouragement, and contributions. Larken Sutherland also provided so much insight and conversation.

Peg Conrad, VP of publications at aha! Process, was amazing as she always is and adapted her schedule to make the book happen. Jesse Conrad was a wonderful editor. Paula Nicolella's design makes the book easy to read, and Amy Perich designed our cover. Carlos Saiz-Perez, director of marketing and strategic digital development, was instrumental in getting the cover designed, as well as the PowerPoint and logos. Finally, and most importantly, I'd like to thank my husband, Tee Bowman, who is VP of sales development and operations. He was so helpful and thoughtful in this process of writing and revising. Thank you, Tee.

Index

[Page numbers in *italics* refer to tables or illustrations.]

problematic, 98
Discrimination
  gender, 77–78
  language, 70–73
  racial, 60–62, 63, 69, 70
  sexual orientation, 66–68
  shame from, 62–63, 66, 68, 70, 73,
    75, 76, 78, 82
Disorders, biochemical, 125, 132–134
Disorganized attachment
  of Columbine shooters, 43
  discipline for, 45
  safe, and dangerous, 39, 40–42, 42,
    45, 85, 108
  students grouped as, 85
Disrespect, 17
Distrust, and trust, 23, 26
Divorce, 129
"Don't You Want to Put Some Makeup
  on? Dealing with Gender and Body
  Discrimination" (Ford), 77–78
Double consciousness, 60–62
"Double Consciousness: Dealing with
  Racial Discrimination" (Auzenne-
  Curl), 60–62
DSM-5. See Diagnostic and Statistical
  Manual of Mental Disorders, fifth
  edition
Du Bois, W. E. B., 60
"Dual-Language, One Choice: Dealing
  with Dual-Language Discrimination"
  (Perez), 70–73

E

Educator. See teachers
Elaine (pseudonym), 8–9
Emoji, 50–51, 94
Emotional baggage
  in classroom, 95–96, 96
  death as, 135
  mother as, 95–96, 109
  parents as, 95–96
Emotional dance
  adults impacting, 107
  teacher regarding, 97, 122–123

Emotional development, 35
  factors impacting, 125
  student stagnation of, 27–28
Emotional issues, 99, 102, 103, 105, 106
Emotional level, 28
Emotional meltdown
  adult response to, 17
  as brain response, 16–17
  calming techniques for, 18–20, 19
Emotional neglect, 129
Emotional noise, 151
  in adult development, 121–122
  on campus, 124
  in classroom, 99, 101, 103, 105, 106,
    123
  from emotional issues, 99, 102, 103,
    105, 106
  in English department, 116
  interventions for, 123–124
  teacher regarding, 97, 99, 101, 103,
    104, 106
Emotional processing, 87, 89, 92
Emotional resources checklist, 7
Emotional response
  prefrontal cortex containing, 16
  tools for, 143
Emotional state, 3–4
Emotional triage, 83, 84–85, 85
Emotional work, 54
Emotions
  female and male tendencies with, 91
  intensity of, 55–56
  naming of, 50–51, 51
  negative, 55
Energy
  contingent, 112, 114
  depleted, 112, 114, 122
  over life span, 113
  responsibilities compared to, 114,
    114–115, 115
  of teachers, 111–115, 113, 114, 115
  in 30s, 113, 113–114, 114
  uses of, 112
English department, 102, 116
Environment, home, 1

About the Author

Ruby K. Payne, Ph.D. is CEO and founder of aha! Process and an author, speaker, publisher, and career educator. She is a leading expert on the mindsets of economic class and on crossing socioeconomic lines in education and work. Payne is recognized internationally for her foundational and award-winning book, *A Framework for Understanding Poverty*, now in its fifth revised edition, which has sold more than 1.8 million copies. Payne has helped students and adults of all economic backgrounds achieve academic, professional, and personal success.

Payne's expertise stems from more than 30 years of experience in public schools. She has traveled extensively and has presented her work throughout North America and in Europe, Australia, China, and India. She has spoken to more than 2 million educators and trained more than 7,000 trainers to do her work. Her speaking engagements have included EARCOS (East Asia Regional Council of Schools) in Malaysia, National Association of School Boards, Central States Bankers Conference, Federal Reserve Board of Governors, Bejing Institute of Education, Harvard Summer Institute for Principals, as well as thousands of individual school districts and campuses.

Payne has written or coauthored more than a dozen books. Recent publications are the revised edition of *Research-Based Strategies: Narrowing the Achievement Gap for Under-Resourced Students,* coauthored with Bethanie H. Tucker, Ed.D., which won the Independent Publishers Bronze Educational Resource Award; *How Much of Yourself Do You Own? A Process for Building Your Emotional Resources,* coauthored with Emilia O'Neill-Baker, Ph.D.; and the third revised edition of *Removing the Mask: How to Identify and Develop Giftedness in Students from Poverty,* coauthored with Paul D. Slocumb, Ed.D. and Ellen Williams, Ed.D. The previous edition of *Removing the Mask* won a gold medal from Independent Publisher Book Awards.

Another major publication is *Bridges Out of Poverty,* coauthored with Philip E. DeVol and Terie Dreussi-Smith, which offers strategies for building sustainable communities. Payne's mission of raising student achievement and overcoming poverty has become a cornerstone for school improvement efforts undertaken by educational districts and Bridges communities across the United States.

Other publications include: *Under-Resourced Learners: 8 Strategies to Boost Student Achievement; Hidden Rules of Class at Work,* coauthored with Don Krabill; *School Improvement: 9 Systemic Processes to Raise Achievement,* coauthored with Donna Magee, Ed.D.; *Crossing the Tracks for Love: What to Do When You and Your Partner Grew Up in Different Worlds; Living on a Tightrope: A Survival Handbook for Principals,* coauthored with William Sommers, Ph.D.; *What Every Church Member Should Know About Poverty,* coauthored with Bill Ehlig; and *Achievement for All: Keys to Educating Middle Grades Students in Poverty,* published by the Association for Middle Level Education (AMLE). *Boys in Poverty: A Framework for Understanding Dropout,* coauthored with *Removing the Mask* collaborator Paul Slocumb, was published by Solution Tree Press and received the Distinguished Achievement Award from the Association of Educational Publishers in the professional development category.

Payne received a bachelor's degree from Goshen College, a Master's Degree in English Literature from Western Michigan University, and her Ph.D. in Educational Leadership and Policy from Loyola University Chicago.

Welcome to the digital era —— of aha! Process ——

With our new web app, you will have access to all our materials, trainings, and webinars in one place under one affordable monthly subscription.

Ebooks

Free Webinars

Online Training on Demand

Live-Streamed Training

For more information visit us at: ahaprocessdigital.com